# FISH ARE EASY

George Hopewell

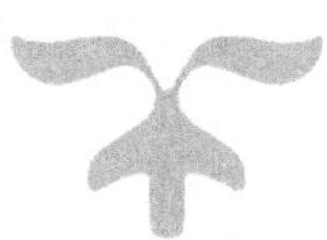

First published 2023
Published by String Publishing



Also by George Hopewell:

*Sliip*
Warm Waters
Warm Waters – the Treacle

ISBN: 978-1-7392800-1-7

*These poems have been written over a long period, starting back in my time as a copywriter in advertising, when I was encouraged to write and publish by Edwin Brock. I am aware how irrelevant poetry is for most people, how pointless poems are and how immaterial poetry is to the world of publishing. Many of these poems were published in various magazines and competitions. Some poems were written in a few days, others honed over a lifetime. Despite the pointlessness of poetry and the prejudice that makes people think publishing poetry is a form of conceit and vanity, my hope is that maybe somebody will get something out of one or two of these poems.*

# CONTENTS

## Sometime

Sometime
I'll drive to a town
with no centre, no sign
where years ago we knew the skyline
(I'll turn up and so will you, at the same time).

We'll find the lane without a map
everything will be behind our backs
like outlaws, we'll cover out tracks
to the house, like a standing stone
on the sand.

There we'll lie without compromise
over a sea we'll open our eyes
hold salt lips to sea light
our tongues will taste
without the lies.

We will unsee the tarnished teeth
nicotine feet, mortal eye
there will be no desire for the next life
we'll wake up to breakfast
and take our time

convinced by courage
at the last view
we'll find we're immaterial
and you'll love me and I'll love you
from every single angle.

**Cut Hand**

I see your cut hand
a slit healing but still
red flanged
a forensic guess of a week?

I hadn't seen it.
For how long
have husband and wife not held hands?
This cut has healed without my
small token of sympathy.

Lovers hold hands
and finger every scrap of skin with messages.
One small touch of tenderness
is too late now
I pat your hand
pretend the skin is perfect.
Remember
when I used to kiss you
better?

## Bluestocking

On the 'DAILY SPORT' hoarding
the blue-stockinged bimbo
'GETS IT EVERY DAY'
but has now got it dribbling with feminist paint.

I have my own blue stocking at work
whose bespectacled intensity and whippet ancestry
are fed on literature
theatre and art.

Paper succulence.

She tells me *all* men compete
*therefore* cannot make friends, *thus* are incomplete.
She herself, makes *deep* friendships with females
who, in gallery tea shops, swap halitosis tales.

So we men can't play a part
we're left dribbling at the paper-stockinged tart.
She may not be in a gallery
but at least she's real art.

## Vale

Hump of earth
one star, smoke clouds fisting along.
I
the featured one
pin-legged and porous-eyed
insect
nipped in the great red grin
the vast swing of the land's red vale.
Ochrous rubble, spike stubble
flint knuckle
run with the run of the wind
land flat with two feet down
boom from the valley's sound.
Listen!
Crab tree
pinned to the wind hill
locks its talon hand
dares me disturb
the burnished turning of the land's
fat sleep.

## Too Few

Suddenly you're told
by the girl in Body Shop's seamless skin
her amethyst eyes winning every prize over yours
in the staring mirror
suddenly everyone's in bloom
except you.

The years collect
like dry shoes in the bottom of the wardrobe.
When it began, in a hot private garden
flesh sponged flesh and stuck on cotton
the start of a never-ending summer
of bare feet.
Days of
tearing off leaves, inhaling pollen
and arching with spreading petals
for the ripe stamen.
Again and again
your heels pressed into lawns and meadows
wringing with the juices of summer.
But that was it
too quick
too soon
too few.

Now you're out of bud
pot-bound and dusty in a house.
Everyone else took lovers
their old tongues are entwining for the last few times
not you
you never exhaled your sweet scent again.
You've forgotten what it's like
to drink nectar all night
in the hothouse.

## Rock Pool

This is our rock pool, pretty as a doily
spring-cleaned twice daily
a cul-de-sac of prawns, small fry
thumbnail crabs and gossamer larvae.
With tiny mouths we peg our claims
count and arrange every grain

filter the sand for gossip.
We do not go far but cling to crevice
crawl with miniature caravans
nook and cranny across our land
dibbling with our forks and knives
it's early to bed and early to rise.

But the cold cistern of the deep
gropes our seams
flushes into our kidney dish invading dreams.
A centrifuge of confusion.
Strange mouths nuzzle our homes, wreck gardens
lift our monuments like stones.

Phosphorescent froth blows in
tales of manta rays and flying fish
mermaids and coral reefs
celebrity sharks
pavements lined with seaweed
soundings from the deep.

We are not deceived
and fix our children in fissures
nibble the tide's watery treats.
In our model village by the sea
we keep to the shallows
cold-shoulder the deep.

## Garlic Lane

Out
when the lane on the hill
slips like black, wet lava
and streams with filtered gravel
washing grass and straw that was once
dung:

A mole
dropped like a velvet purse
from cat's mouth
or drowned
its nose pressed into fine clean sand:

The evening garlic lane
breathes moisture like a lung
steams and recuperates
welded to earth by the weaning sun.

Once you have mastered the sky
felt its breath
diluted its taste – blue upon blue
held its gaseous height about your head
then you can master the trees:

Trembling in the green diamonds of their leaves
they touch
soft cheek against soft cheek
hush and brush their shivering shapes
fur forests on the hill.

Only then can you master the hard white sun
falling failing calling:
There is an end.

## Maple Morning

Behind these obscured windows
families sleep
transplanted from week to weekend.

A slot of sunlight aims
invades
and the lawns smoulder with dew
walls stand their ground, absorbing
aching
and leaves bag their first skinful
tippling the liquor without a sound.
Trees finger windows
and soil sweats, incubating
blood, bone and bedding plants.

Inside the curtain-lit rooms
mothers and fathers tangle in love
children, strangled in sheets
retrieve balls from garage roofs
in dreams dowsed with mortality.
All is deliquescing, delivering
thumb to mouth, seed to womb
shoots of green searching.
The seedlings are pricking up
the stems are thickening.

Now the children's eyes ignite
ray-gunned by the sun.
The morning is drying, stretching
its chrysalis
lawns render their spit
first curtains are drawn.
The houses stare, deaf, mute
fixing their faces for the day's rotation
every atom a sunrise older
every cell enslaved to the prevailing sun.

## Lido

First, small feet dipped, titbits
in the pool.
Appetizers.
Then calves
balancing thighs wide as goblets.
Winter flesh flakes into fillets of light
nipped by Lycra seams
stretched between buttocks
taut as trampolines.
Stomachs submerge, sensitive udders
breasts goose-pimple and levitate
finally shoulders lose the debate
leaving hands guillotined dry.

Some are seals
and dive between dainty hands and dainty feet
great streamlined torpedoes.
Others are eels
that submerge and emerge
hair slung back like weed
glistening foreheads.
No perms, powder, paint, perfumes
honest women
peeled as prawns.

Not one splashes or laughs
all swim in a sea of thought
distilled day-dreams
green pod, green pool, green submarine sight
water tickling and grating light.
They emerge amphibians
in jungle air
gallons to spare
3-D in all dimensions.

Were I a fly on the wall of the shower
I'd spy through steamed up compound eye
that one last peel of clammy cloth

a second skin that enveloped so much
dropped
on the tiles
like a balloon just popped
the immensity of women
naked as birth.

## Basingstoke Shopping Centre

The pub blows hot stale breath
fog in shreds
supermarket mantras
cling wrap air
bodies, chests, vests
wringing underarm

Lamppost weather.
The coughing stubble
phlegm on the street
chip paste kisses
twist of the feet.

Pigeon slips
club foot
stabs stubs.
Lovers snog
embrace each other's
wet weather leathers
lather at the mouth.

Mystic tramp curls into
tight cramp on bench
fingers
dustbin dinners
tilting liquor.
Footsteps squirt
staring at each other.
Dead eye
damp fever on the slab.

## Congratulatory Peach

The peach
I bought
for you
to eat
you
ate
casually
as if I hadn't bought it specially
juice running down your cheek.
You slim and lovely
my love lonely.

Empty
the room
the head
the page.
Too comfortable
I
in my comfortable chair
you just there
all
of the time.

## Predator

Barracuda bitch is stainless steel.
She circles her prey, sleek with roe
lets his eyes taste her from tail to toe
then kicks water
cuts in for the kill

lips barbed with lust
eyes wide as bathyspheres
she flaunts the flag of her fin
her thrusting jaw
a visor grin of teeth.

Her tail slides with sex.
She spits his dull feathers, a feeble lure
twists her spine
then gaffs his flanks in a bloody vice
takes her man whole

coupling like a duel
mouth against mouth
gill against gill
she jams him up her cloaca
pumps him to the rhythm of the sea.

Until his wasted seed
is milk
in the suspension of the ocean
and her eyes have drawn curtains
over his mind.

## September Funeral

There can be nothing in this funeral
but the body loose
in the coffin.

There can be nothing in the sky
but sightless eyes
and heavy march the restless feet
in anguished time.

How calm is the mind
that sleeps still
and like a yacht loosed across the sky
breathes cold night in
lies back
rests
and dies.

September – sweet child
that stilled the evening's air
and threaded mist in morning trees
tipped leaves upon new soil.

**Paddling in Unison**

Sometimes there is nothing
no love to keep under the pillow
safe in the sarcophagus.
The dreams are over
like ghosts caught forever
under vinyl wallpaper.
As weak as watered whisky
you scarcely keep going
but canoe on
together

laughing wonderfully at the dinner party
smelling the scent of other women
you behaved, passed the salt in public
and watched the pivot of laughter swing
up and down the table
like a tired pendulum
beating out the same thoughts
and jokes
waiting to go

home
to a room like an abandoned chess game
the babysitter asleep.
Nip small comfort from the children's
salted cheeks
down a whisky
and hug your husband like an old dog
canoe on
out of habit
go to bed to read

or make love
as he tightens the autumn skin over your cheeks
like a plastic surgeon.
A woman growing old
is the saddest thing
when the mouth turns to rag

the eyelids fold in
but together you'll canoe on

up this narrowing stream
lying in bed with
no one
to meet in the uninhabited garden
no one
to walk the cliffs in the evening.
All you can do
is canoe on
paddling in unison.

## Puppies

Black boys
bean bags
muscle boys in roly-poly skins
damp dog-licked sweet pickle
bellies and crotches
pink as black man's palms.

Open gullets
a fish or baby bird's
mouse-trap gums
but Mum's too tired
tits hang like folded crepes
the puppies hinge
bloodsuckers on the line.

Shovel-nosed replicas
we are the septuplets
eyes nearly, blearily waking up
when
almost by chance
one wet hot haggis pops the pack
sausage rolls from the basket
hits the linoleum floor
on his teddy bear back.

A belated discovery this.
Almost by chance
I, too
pulled the curtains back
nosed cold glass
snorkelled out.

> Plants swaying like polyps
> a breeze of mulched grass
> things darting behind trees
> night pressing my facemask.

In the blood-sweet wine and plastic straw

six tails twitch in dreams
the seventh is flat out on the kitchen floor
washed up on some vast
linoleum beach.

> The eagle's claw, crow's ice-pick beak
> rubber roar of pterodactyl wings
> the prodding, stabbing from above
> pellets our big boy by the stove.

Night retracts.
Water reforms to watered glass
a drop tracing a path
like an ant choosing this, choosing that.
The puppy spreads his finger legs
a pensioner on ice.
I too, retract
toss the puppy back
with the rest.

**Old Friends**

Old friends.
We trod paths
founded and broke homes
created small dynasties
crowded with new
soft-skinned players

who grew
more beautiful
than their mothers
with whom we used to
(when we cross-reference)
kick Autumn leaves

unclothe in halls of residence.
Now at Guy Fawkes parties
we eat their recipes
being good team players
we never mention those
whose names were earmarked

for millions
or those who found
cures to world diseases.
They curse us with their success
feeding doubt to our eyes
our failed ambition.

So we hope that somehow
somewhere
they paid a price
dying
dull, divorced or, preferably
ignorant.

## The Face

The design has the skin slit twice
for two glass eyes
once for a mollusc that lives
between the lips inside.
See how the muscles exercise
occluding passages from soul
messages of code
flicking on, off
masks of compromise.
The eyelids tremble in anger
for here is the foundation of fear:
You are pulling the threads of your own eyes
blind.

I look to the micro spasms
of the mouth
as you stretch fine purple lips
tender with their net of nerves.
There is treason in this team
you are pronouncing words you do not mean
like a speech therapist practising
but I can guess at the unseen.
We are all amateur
lip readers.

So we decode these plasticine frames
probe
the way to a phantom scene
opening trapdoors we spy
the occult landscape inside.
The threat of another mind
is of the lightless zone
the extrusion of a soul
through a face
full of holes.

## Third Christmas

Cast out of the inn
over a pint and a sandwich
the other man's child

spent its months guessing its parentage
trusting a mother's love, knowing
why her old body had

ached so hard
for a lover's sperm
to be buried in her womb

forecasting its weight, its sex, its suckling
at those new taut breasts.
But in its absence, at a clinic

birth was turned down.
Once radiant, the good mother
shrunk, bled to death.

Another miscalculation
another wrong person.
Spurn life, spurn hope

send back love.

## Mongolian Wild Horse

My currency was swaps
my language numbers 1 to 50
sliding in a blue embossed
Harrogate Toffee tin.
I can still smell the virgin
tea cards
from Brooke Bond

kept an album (PRICE SIXPENCE)
each rectangle blank
begging a card to be stuck in
safe as a bank.
Just before supermarkets
when mums left babies outside shops
and the lady at the till always had swaps

but no one had
the Mongolian Wild Horse

until there it was in the playground.
We crowded around, glimpsed the holy ink
mouthing the caption in sync
hurting from our own incomplete
albums.
*I'll give you a hundred cards*
*for it.*

So set is the habit of looking to the next
I'll still dream of winning the pools
on my death bed
but no row of bank balance noughts
or adulterous sexual intercourse
will ever be coveted half as much
as the Mongolian Wild Horse.

## Food

It began with nibbling
testing our tongues with titbits.
Kicked out of kitchens, we ate raw
snacked on the back seats of buses
salivated on street corners
hid away takeaways in bedrooms
but nothing satisfied us.

We began to wolf our meals
junk food, midnight feasts
gorging bedsit fish 'n' chips
going back for seconds.
We loitered by restaurant menus
ate between meals
dreamt of full English breakfasts.

Learning to cook
we garnished, discovered herbs
paused between courses
experimented.
Food was art and we were connoisseurs
we ate well
but missed a good blowout.

Then the portions shrank.
Steak and kidney once a week
cordon bleu on Friday night, Indian
or Chinese for a birthday treat.
New recipes, but the same ingredients
we worked harder on presentation
took evening classes to stimulate digestion.

Soon it was low-calorie, oven-ready
diets and bite-size rations
vegetables were barely thawed
the microwave ruled the kitchen.
We frisked the freezer for something seasoned
but survived on aperitifs

that grew weaker and weaker.

Now I eat in front of the telly
my eyes are bigger than my belly
no one wants to cook for me
with jaded palate, flatulence, over-acidity.
So it's meals on wheels or frozen peas
all that's left of my bon appetite
is cup-a-soup gastronomy.

## Gully

He took three days to set it
underfed, Irish
fucking every word
bedding ceramic pipes
on cushions of mortar

like a mortician laying a dead lover
infinite care, dignity
mud up to his shoulder
stroking cement seams
smooth as granite streams.

Soil would slip like an otter
no toilet tissue or turds snagging
as the great architect craps
looks up to vaults of light
that were once his maps.

He couldn't give a fuck
that ten foot below
art
is transporting
his muck.

## You

I saw the sad softness of your neck
bend your head.
I smelt its sweat
velvet-lipped its quivering form
snuffed dark the rank roots of your hair
dug deeper than the rest.

I drew a finger on the line
that cleaves your breasts up from your chest.
I inched your corduroy skirt
- two shining knees.

I ran the dead bells
of your two daft plaits.
I smoothed the limp seam of your thighs
- flesh from birth's cool night.

## Concrete

Mixing a mountain
sand, cement, gravel.
Little girl cries
a pain in the elbow.
Water bursting walls
lake in an extinct volcano.
Little girl
goes to the doctor.

Grey cement polluting
tide running, eroding.
Little girl's
in hospital.
Weight of concrete
slides off shovel.
Little girl
further investigations.

Heavy shovelling
buckets of authority.
Little girl
diagnosed leukaemia.
Pour it, tamp it
smooth the surface.
Little girl's
home from hospital.

Hot sun dries
to firm sand tide.
Little girl
little white coffin.
Overnight sets
to a hard white step.
Little girl's footprint
cast in concrete.

## Big Cats

You catch me ogling young women
and lie back yawning, ignoring.
Is your old husband contemplating
straying
from the family pride
again?

But who can love these kittens
with their soft pink ribbons
as they prowl the malls in brownie packs
mewling for attention.
With their coquette tails and stroke-me necks
and deodorized little arses
who's fussed about these pampered pets
these perfumed pettish
kitty cats.

I can only love big cats
who, with proven prowess
have shagged, ridden birth and growled
on their backs.
They shoved out blood-stained babies
squeezed milk from blue-veined titties
only big cats can bring a wildebeest down
dead in his tracks.
Look at them lying proudly on the savannah
laughing in their gynaecological mafias.
Who's going to play with kittens
when you've a tried and tested
cat?

## Condom

Intriguing to schoolgirls
this escargot
slips from its foil
furled in its ring.
Unroll

when filling.
You're not really sliding
epithelium upon epithelium
just thinly disguising
blunt nerve endings

as it keeps you guessing
kissing through polythene.
And after you're done
it's doubly disgusting
a disposable, medical

sausage skin.
And tiny nothings
with strange compulsion
convulse in microscopic
seas of plankton

as the bubble in the teat
keeps it floating
dancing round and round
telling everyone
you must have done

something.

**Sideboards**

Remember when
we girls giggled at pregnant women
as proof they'd had copulation
and pondered on which direction
erections were supposed to erect in
(and no one ever mentioned

masturbation).
And we boys only knew each other
from top to bottom in the shower
armpits, cocks, pubes and farting
(and none of our sheets
ever needed starching).

And we hoped for
electric razors for Christmas
or knickers smaller than navy blue knickers
from mothers who never said 'Jesus'
and fathers who never wore
denim or canvas.

Until after the summer one came back
and swore he'd had a girl in a haystack
and we knew for certain
he wasn't a fraud
by his new, rectangular
sideboards.

**Slugs**

Under a bunged and bulging sky
I take the strimmer to the allotments
a paddy field, grass thigh high
dock, nettles, thick wristed giants
wrestling, untrammelled, for a month.

Call it a 'Black and Decker'
but you watch it massacre
the propeller stings like a laser
whole rain forests are flicked away.
This is no manicure
no trendy trim for a city garden
this is them and us

slugs and guts.

Big as pork tenderloins
supine as plucked tongues
they stretch orange hovercraft skirts
arrogant, repulsive, slobs.

Vengeance is mine
the whip hovers, shrieks
as they shrink like steaks, lower periscopes
then explode, hot water bottles
decapitate, ooze orange, purple
colostomies.

I have killed
with salt napalm (they squirm in froth)
and poison bombs (they curl like sun-dried bananas)
but this is no TV war
death is instant, horrible
within the length of an arm.

Whose aesthetic
to give gut reactions
where there's no guts

to tongue tongues in love
plug kids with jelly baby plugs
dress snails on restaurant tables
not these

rubber fuckers.

## Ruby Wedding

Here, every couple loves deep as a walk to Watersmeet
or tea by the sea at Rhossili.
The graves are booked, twin headsets
for two single beds, touching fingertips
over a Teasmade.
The years have papier-mâchéd into masks
of marriage
but laughter bleaches the groynes of teeth
as the champagne tickles the ribs.

The husbands
huddle like boys in the showers
laughing beyond the official hours
they minute the dead
then drink to keep the old beak
absent.
They still hide a few secrets
but shuffle, dependent
on their wives' surveillance

who, on chairs in the sun
network couplets of names
on note-paper, headed by pets
and places.
Memory is the agenda:
Counting children in county places
painting by numbers old faces
conversations like recipes, tried and tested
with a few, just a few, spicy ingredients.

As the wives queue for discounts at the buffet
the men loosen their ties
then, refilling their glasses nimbly as spies
they return to the army wedding
young men in a Stanley Spencer painting
raising ceremonial swords at a church
forty years ago.

## Phone Book

Open this book to a nightmare inventory.
An entomologist
has inscribed line after line
of pin-prick women and matchbox men.

A 9-point memory
gibberish to a Martian
a million insects pinned in trays
with no further information

just cover to cover
of family specimens
house flies, larvae
an anonymous Domesday

of human pestilence.

There's no satisfaction
no illustrations
in this paperback list
no live action.

makes your skin crawl
the nits on your neck prick
rack after rack of pierced thorax
an infinite A to Z.

Out there is me
in my glass case, a single entry
a one line label of ink
my microdot autobiography.

Ring me, I'm under 'B'
I hope to be in **bold** by '93
unless I tear my pin right out
and go ex-directory.

## Sky

Tonight
the clouds are coal dust
sprinkled and sifted
soot upon a thin paper sky.

The leaves of my horse chestnut
hang like napkins
and a star's tweezered light
eats a cell in the eye.

Dreams of the future
whose house of flint
and garden where you will sit with green stems
mourning green dusk
and blossom still the air
holding its vacuum breath
saying:
Why can't I look at the sky?

With some recollection
somewhere
of an oval window of light
stacked oak library shelves
and a blot of bat
flipping and twisting
in the water blue sky.

## Doing

In our road of company cars
is a house barred by a jungle
creepers wire the windows
neighbours
point fingers at his garden.

There he works
professing to clear the ground
but relapsing to picking up bits
like an archeologist
blue china, clay pipes, bones
a fork twitcher
bent on detail
no grand scheme of landscape design
he picks up rocks and sets them down.

Thus he opts for failure
concentrates on a pocket handkerchief arena
contemplating the jungle
when there's a need to slash and burn.
We would advise weed killer
a JCB, a sit-on mower
but, in fear of wearing someone worn
stay dumb

in fear of presuming what is right
is *doing*
like some business plan
as if it mattered to get it all done
in time.

## Grandchildren

They come with sharpened sticks
prodding, goading, baiting the bear
who doesn't feel like dancing.

Every mouth nips, yelping for reaction
as I pirouette, manacled by questions
a bear with a sore head
swiping in all directions.

There's no hugs left in this bear garden.

I trail their mothers in National Trust houses
who, with agonizing erudition
advertise their devotion
(terriers under heel)
tongues electric with the zeal of
e d u c a t i o n.

To these offspring
everything's a zoo
only the biggest and best will do.
So let me be relegated to
something stuffed and unfashionable
a small-town museum, dusty and dowdy
no buttons to press, no bars
to poke fingers through.
A boring bear
in his Victorian drawing room.

The mothers and T-shirt terriers can rush by
leaving me
in blissful taxidermy.

## Hug in Mousehole

Always by water
we drive the black lanes of Cornwall
caught inside a car.
Above those hard stones and black air
your arms hold the whole weight of the sky
and nervous stars sipping at the harbour.
Water has that selfless urge
to pull into the black hole of the retina
the whole damn weight of the universe.
The weak stare of a star
(erasing any thought about the next and the next move)
draws us out onto the theatre of rock.
Exposed
we recoil from the habits of home
we escaped with our lives somehow.

Always by water
whose heartless lips grope and fold the sand
grind the wreck, sink it in depth.
Cold chapel of death, left in disgrace
now a dirty tourist place
those fishermen drawn into the sea like lead
by her cruel but certain fate.
I can't break your grasp
I don't know why your arms are breaking my side
cold hearted lover.
Set inside this rock, inside the granite's guts
here I can hide, caught in the fearless tide
this human hug.

Always by water
no mason gave these rocks their home
one winter's day, unknown
they cleaved from cliff, drew together
then ground in time
one slit where the barnacles congregate and hide
is a clue for future tides
to work these rocks apart.

I know that you are mine
your arms, your hard ribs, buttressed against mine
mine, in time.
In time, too
we tourists take home one piece of Cornish granite for the patio
where it lies, unremembered and alone
like a drab animal in a zoo.
Even our children's varnished shells
lose their soft shine.
We're all under the same sky
but at home, we hide
we no longer know.

Always by water
we're advising each other where to park
when it rains, which pub after dark
our children test the winds with crisp packets
the sand with surface art.
The sea's temper tantrums are too weak to shift our rock
but let rock be honest and blunt, arm itself against barefoot
scrape skin to the bone
and where our shoes have worn our rock to land
let it wipe our groping act from the sand.
The sea's acid pleasure wipes clean the arena
leaves Japanese gardens around our rock.
Let us sweep up our tourist muck
(like a gardener's thumb cleans aphids off a leaf.)
we are pleased to leave our secrets with the tide.

Always by water
I see the lanes and paths where you were a farmer's girl
walking up from Lamorna
where one slip is to reinforce the cliff's permanent threat
of death.
The succinct hitting of skull against rock.
You're a tourist now, don't lose your head
you could fall like all the rest
the sea shan't have the weight of your hard skull
no sea shall wreck our Mousehole hug
your granite caste against my throat

the sea sipping my neck, granite chest versus endless sea.
Hold me against this terror
mouth to mouth with the cold grouper.
Let the sea slip her freezing fingers in
and grind off a thin skin with her sandy teeth
to separate me.

Always by water
the sea will never lift these rocks
the sea cannot lift the love locked
in these bales of stone.
What men gave their lives with gristle, rope and bone
in defence of these rocks?
You and I passed so close in the black harbour
locked inside the hug.
We hear the fractured days let go
but I am scared to look beyond the sand between my toes
you lever my head to the view
I never knew you were so strong.
The harbour night and terrifying tide threaten:
Let the sea in.

Pitched on the sand with a family
in your hugging harbour
I focus on a gull, carefree in the sky
and favour the incoming tide.
You're tied to me, you'll grind into me,
in time.

## It's got to be somewhere

It's got to be somewhere.
So we search
under clothes, duvets
envelopes.
Something has been put on top
it's disappeared, underneath.
It's got to be somewhere
but it isn't.
Now it's more than mislaid
it's lost.

It's got to be somewhere.
Amongst all those years
we search.
It's got to be somewhere
somewhere concealed
displaced, not lost.
But it isn't. It was
a set of photographs we never took.
It isn't somewhere
it never was.

## Party Wall

The wall has sliced like a mirror
two halves
they have the silver side
we are matt, windowless.
The sun planned this trick with a protractor
lighting half the world
a full smile on their sundial
ours in full shadow.

They with their polished cutlery
a Burmese cat basking
on the dust of the baby grand.
Six immaculate balconettes
carpets warm enough to make love on.
Behind their hand-printed wallpaper
they party with vines, friendly bees
lollo rosso and sun-dried tomato.

Nine inches away in the undercliff
we stretch necks to exits like prisoners
lie on floors of lead
sheets damp as tea towels.
We press ears to our plaster
hear the beat of their Bose subwoofer
drill fingernails to ladder their long legs
scratch off those dancing sequins

squeeze wasps
from jam holes in our doughnuts.
Train them to sting
on the party side of the wall.

## Fish are Easy

To the great white shark we came to confess
Fish are easy, he said, easy as sin
come little fishes, don't be distressed
begin your confession, begin.

*As children we over-fed the goldfish*
*it gas-bellied upside-down in the dish*
*we chloroformed frogs, pinned their hearts*
*sautéed sticklebacks in jam jars*
*sawed eels in half, then gave chase*
*tore hooks from gudgeons, disembowelled dace*
*dissected crania of dead dogfish*
*fed tuna rolls to live tunny fish*
*squeezed roe from sturgeons, drank elver sperm*
*crucified and drowned a million unwilling worms*
*massacred sharks with machetes and guns*
*imprisoned dolphins in dolphinariums*
*parted the thighs of a singing mermaid*
*held her head underwater and explained:*

*Fish are easy.*

Absolved, he said, well done my men.
Come follow me, my fishy friends
come to the slaughter, you need not pretend
fish eat fish, that's all there is
so sin and sin again.

So we swam in circles underneath
breathed his red water, loved his cold heat.
Did we see the blue marlin in the deep?
No
we gutted, gutted, gutted.

## Wine Cellar

Claustrophobic vaults
under the burden of a closed dark shop
this wine cellar's sawdust and gauze light
buff the daylight grain from your neck
and the pressings from your chin
so your face becomes pastel
sixteen again.
With the beer inside me cold as a drain
and leaking into my blood
my head is overripe with emotion
and I love, I love.
Of course I'm not drunk
I might be a bit scaly from work
the pages are ready and open
my resolve has been beaten up.
Of course I'm not drunk
I'm racked between
what has been
what might have been
and what might be.

Press-ganged into the present.

Men in suits order after-work meat
take their jackets off
laugh away their wives
and rub knees
with girls from the office
over their candle-lit thighs.

Of course I'm not drunk
I'm press-ganged into the present
running over fields
happy
filthy happy.

## The Established

The cathedral
a stone canyon
we sit surrounded by the dead
in this vast granite volume
of coughs (small rocks hitting the precipice below).
The waterfall trickling in the corner
is someone's sermon.

They kneel
governors of this and that
they who own.
Shoes of scarred saddle
leather soles thick with wear
as they pray
they know God off by heart.
Pin-stripes are nicely jaded
coats stretched on genteel shoulders
seriously worn elbows.
Elders
whose necks and bellies bear
the power through the ages
men who never doubted
only ever had one set of clothes
to put on.

Voices of charmed resonance
sing hymns
for Queen, Country
and the healing of the nations
through Jesus Christ our Lord
Amen.
Some mouths are magnificent in confidence
others caught in the half smile of the aristocrat
with that twist of beneficent Christian doubt.
They have licked their white hair
and sharpened their eyebrows
there's nothing semi-detached here
just oak studies

grandsons in blazers
large cotton underwear.

Across the aisle
the pack of wives struggle to find the correct page
wriggle their feet in coloured shoes.
They wear the usual hats.

They live longer than mortal man
in estates permanent as cathedrals
and laws eternal as the God
who bows his white hair with them.
They render no one evil for evil.
For the established
the burden of patronage is immense.

## Red Light District

They are strangely beautiful
with smooth skins and fine limbs
and shaven crotches
suggesting no wear and tear
no deterioration in their female swellings
just a trifle weary.
I suppose they are only prodded and pawed
being screwed is less wearing than scrubbing floors.

In each door
they are transfigured
in ultraviolet light.
Her phosphorescent lingerie
makes me believe she's clean and bright as the moon
her smiling teeth and wiggles
and weighted dancing nipples
make me presume
she'll do anything for me.
I'm flattered by the pout she throws at me
gives me more eye contact than I've had in a week
even though I know that's how it's supposed to be
even though I know it all stinks
she's still a sexy lady.

If I was to open her glass door
see her curtain discreetly drawn
find her alien nails on my zip
would I find a woman down on her luck
down on her knees
or a cold-eyed manipulator of the male bits?
It's an odd thing, sex
how is it different from, say, massaging your legs
or washing your feet?
But it would be nice to touch
those long silk stockings and tiny white knickers
and lift those breasts out of that gossamer bra
(How carefully you choose your working clothes)
but I move on, of course

to the SEX shops full of plastic penises
videos of buttocks and purple slits
and erections as large as cucumbers.
Here, it's easier to throw stones.
I don't wish to be drawn on the exploitation of women
I want to return to my hotel room
rest my weary legs
and, maybe, wash my feet
but a wheelchair has tracked dogshit across the reception
and the maid is scrubbing it
down on her knees.

## Structural Engineer

With grandiose displays of hoarding
he builds
crisscross cats' cradles, climbing frames
where once there was air.

Engineers by desire and design
steel from frail foundations
aims high, scaffolds against
collapse.

Inserts prefabricated walls
course after course, concrete
to squeeze out sky.
All will be clad, all is

façade
the ultimate metaphor.
Composite stone is his compromise
clip-on architecture his disguise

to keep out sunlight.
He who builds bigger, builds better
but his impressive exterior
is all entrance, all mouth and marble.

Inside, an empty warehouse
terra firma without earth
every floor identical
every face mere décor.

TO LET, short lease
open-plan, incomplete.
The shadows compete
as the sun passes his vacancies.

## The Cordless

Days of cerebrum and cerebellum.
Everyone's articulate now
talking telephones
with texted conversations
ready-to-assemble sentences
of cordless communication.

They all speak the lingo, systems
of laser-perfect diction
networking buttons
for hands-on implementation.
Their telepathy's impeccable
brain stems so compatible

just don't give me any more of your
answer-phone answers
your app-fed intuition
orthodox cognition.

Too much has been extinguished
for this lap-top generation.
We may be obsolete
but you're beyond resuscitation.
Oh, go on
talk, talk
clak, clak,
f-function.

## Hagfish

*The Hagfish is a slimy eel*
*he'll wait 'til you are down*
*then rasp his way in thru your arse*
*and eat your viscera warm and brown*
*and when you're just about to die*
*out he'll swim to find*
*another worker with juicy bowels*
*to continue his miserable kind.*

The ratchet clicks
the calendar rips
another day's in the bin.
God, agog with indifference
spreads another virus for sustenance
as you reveal your defences to him.
When frisked for tomorrow's workday sorrows
your underwear's looking grim
so you shave, shower, grab one dreaming hour
until the alarm breaks your neck again.
Time is temporal, you're dreaming and guessing
whether it's morning or evening, then
you're sitting on your suit in your traffic-choked route
you've no secret thoughts to reel in.
One way to keep feeling
is to stare at the ceiling and think
love and sex and sin
but the gnats at work hurt like cheap fireworks
and you can't hear yourself for the din
as your colleagues arrive, they lick your wounds like flies
and craftily lay eggs under your skin.

The Hagfish is slight but he takes a deep bite
tearing out kidney, liver and spleen
you flee, a refugee
to the cold lavatory
you pray, but he preys on inside.
You never did really pass their test
at least you never gave in

but by the end of the week the Hagfish is sleek
and your ulcers are piled in the bin.
Filling the spaces with the requisite phrases
smiling in sentences to fill empty pages
the Hagfish is a glutton for sin.

Suddenly it's all slipped down the pipe
little Haggy has had his fill
last thing at night and first thing in the morning
he opens your bowels for the kill.
You've had all the warnings, postponed all the feelings
you've felt it tug but hadn't the guts to reel in.
The internal predator who loves soft-centred workers
is now getting ready to swim.

## Issue

*Here I go, winding*
*up the band again*
*tighter tighter*
*ready to jump the bungee*
*(snap the elastic, blow the gasket)*
*over the top to ecstasy!*

A million pinheads wriggle
in their cuckoo spit
wimping for a whiff of egg.
Boys and girls, we have left you for dead
stranded on the river bed
(caught in the sieve of a sheet
or jammed up the teat of a rubber bulkhead).

For those who cry 'SPERMICIDE'
at cods' roes in the night
let caviar be spread, pips be spat
and a million grains of rice be shat.

For tissue's the only issue
you put on the light
and wipe 'em up, half alive
a million dead, no inquest, no autopsy

so what's the issue
the batteries recharge daily?

*So haul up the bungee*
*Yo Yo Yo Yo*
*I'm ready to jump*
*I'm ready to blow*
*prime the pump, look out below!*

Plunge, bounce
and let the issue go.

## Statistics

In her head
the artery ballooned and popped
on Monday she was there
on Tuesday she was not.

That stopped us doing this and that
our jokes became quite gravitas
you may as well go out, get pissed
when God chucks darts, it's hit and miss.

We found a 'Which' of used parts
hoses, valves, gaskets and hearts.
Whoever signs a donor card
could be next in the breaker's yard.

Yet every morning we turn the key
the engine comes on magically
only the statistics of the actuary
show those who fail the M.O.T.

It's all been said, the old insight
annihilation – terrible but trite.
You just go over it again and again
when it's one of you, not one of them

who's won the pools of no bye-bye.
This coloured band, no hair to tie
a hidden hand, no ring to hide
a body in a box, no spares inside.

## Babysitting

Inside the chapel of this home
the cat is sleeping, unconscious
of whose human lap it heats
exhaling a small gust of cat breath.
Upstairs, the syncopated breathing
through bedroom doors.
Check out these beautiful sleepers,
unconscious, open-mouthed, weighted arms.

Every corner and cupboard is a potpourri
of these lives
a secret documentary on display.
The vodka in the kitchen
a gear from an extinct Spirograph
the toenail on the hearth
the calendar on the carpet
and woodlouse carapace.

A vast collection of used-by dates.

Disclosures of struggle
in the bank statement by the computer
the strange creams on the bathroom shelf
and the underwear
on the floor of the bedroom.
Every object silent and squealing
with tales
I do not wish to hear.

Babysitter voyeur
having to witness
this still life
a mystic burglar
who prowls
stealing judgements
from this suffocating
home.

## The Deep

Down here is a cageless world
murk, dark
and an underfog.
We slide

until our welds crack.
It was Kant who turned this bathysphere
inside out.
Those fish, he said, are inside
not out. So we pretend
watch fish bones descend
through sea thick as molten glass
cushion onto silt without a sound.

Down to the still
where, with slack cables
we test the thrill of weightlessness
lure, like anglerfish
distant candles
shivering on thin batteries.

We learn
but, on our return
find laughter.
The flotilla's having fun
windsurfing, water-skiing
gibing at us.

This is the risk
that we who sink
cannot find the surface
and all these coloured sails
cannot
reel us up.

## Librarian

A long drawer of oak
brass handle, tincture of archive
a fan of cards tilts *en bloc*
the records of an old bibliophile.

Delve in the back, where birth's copperplate
and school's maladroit type
register kiss-chase, nose-bleeds and love.
Rendezvous ringed in turquoise ink
a few asterisks; *college, *marriage
then a logjam of work.

How quickly the drawer weighed with cards
volumes clogged the shelves.
Dirt from years of browsing fingers
has rubbed dog-ears;
promise that revealed
too little to remark upon

too much
not worth the paper it's printed on.
You never plucked up courage
to chuck out the rubbish
(better a handful of pamphlets
than a library of laminated covers)

for, over the years, books close ranks
trap leaves of nostalgia
and many, so loyal on the shelf
turn out to be *trompe-l'oeil.*
Fame gives a decorative spine
for cowardice in the archive.

But here, slipped in the cards, is a piece of paper
an *aide-mémoire* from a young pretender
forgotten but familiar.
It's torn edge, exhumed, recalls
pages left, unfiled

in the bottom drawer.

These you remember
as you turn the final twist of brass
withdraw the skewer. That one steel spine
held it all together.

## The Outside

At night, I walk to the sink
with the mastery of a blind man
eyes in a velvet bag
fingers in a lucky dip of soot.
I find the shell of the chair
armour of the radiator
an abrupt wall.
My map's in synch
everything is just where I think.
You have to be brave to be blind

brave to believe daylight
is all there is. This weak rainbow
we filch from the mists outside.

Things unseen
glide
with their extra ears and eyes
watch
as we push through froth we cannot feel
raise eyes to colossi invisible.

## Frontier

The sea is rabid with froth
waves beach
somersault, trip
thrash, slavering on the sand
insanely superior to man

who, on the edge of the sea
is a splinter from the land.
Homo erectus, his bipedal stance
feeble as a hairgrip
a foreign body the sea snorts out.

Families in plantations of towels
camp on a contour, sightless under windbreaks.
In the froth, a school of porpoises dance
weaving water, black spears, flashing in parabole
underbellies caught in the resin of a standing wave

then return to the deep, unearthly
green as evolution.
They glanced not once at the land
edging the ocean
beach, café, lifeboat station
(whose frontier?)
but, laughing in their lungs
plunged into an underworld.

As the sea wipes its boundaries
we dabble, peer, trespass
in the shallows
floating the abys we risk vertigo
hang, legs kicking.
Our surfboards and snorkels
pathetic prostheses
in a borrowed world.

## Love Letters

Burning is the way
white paper to a black delicacy
a thorough chemistry

all tunes transcribed
in a miniature hell.
Blue tongues metamorphosing

every key to ash
every signature to parchment.
To avoid exhumation, crush

and the tunes you thought would be
in your children's hearts
are lost from every mouth

the lover's name can't be
sweated from dreams by a truth drug
or dealt in the heat of an argument.

Cremation is all, burn them
musician, music, song.
Be guiltless as a crematorium.

## Helicopter

Outside the glory illustrated box
the shrunken toy dimmed your eyes
but when the rotors spun
you flew it round the skies.

A miniscule product
naff as Vietnam
from a cast of thousands
fabricated in Taiwan.

*Then a big bum sat*
*the rotor blade trapped*
*flesh against plastic*
*fractured like a matchstick.*

The childless out in pubs
eating pizzas by candlelight
know not the evenings spent
shaping rotors for a test flight.

For here is the terror of love;
the cry in the night, the broken part
the drilling, the gluing
the irreparable heart.

## Bluebottle

That evening you kept us from loving
by revving your engine
scrambling all over the air
ricocheting round the lampshade's
wall of death.
I'll crack your carapace
you boy racer
glue you to the wallpaper
with your own turbocharged
entrails.

In the morning you're waiting by the window
engine cold.
We outstare one another
my tai chi palm closes
on your fuel tank
a perfect petrol blue.
Your eyes crystallise me
in a thousand wing mirrors.
PAX.
No more wheelies, no more fight.
I open the window
police you out.

## Bathroom

Outside
the wind beats its black cloak
unleashes a birch hand.
Safely inside
water runs from the tap
a giant applause.
Chemical bathroom!
Television has killed the art
of lying in the bath.
I can hear its tell-tale pap
but am good at creeping out
after dark.

Immersion.
I am gelatine in the bath
a wet and soft and perfumed rat.
My feet are flat on wool
then out
heel marks on the grass.

The sky swings its silver swag
a whipping entrail
in a madman's grasp.
A newspaper cat bounds between the lamps
unwrapping silence.

Outside
I am all fear
bilious bowels, whispering ears
too many dry sailing leaves
skidding on concrete ground.

Inside
through a window of black glass
I see your corpse
slumped on no-man's-land.
Not dawn? Not sky?

Fire flinches in the grate
porcelain, porous
embers chase
weak fluorescence in the brain
thoughts diminishing
hot coal to cold ash
by the morning.

Sleep.
The room, reassuringly perpendicular
bed soft as a rag.
A tap's drip
pops its skin.

I sleepwalk
stalk
the sleeper on the bed
slip over the edge
down some dark vein in my head.
Between the curtains
a thin ghoul, luminescent grey
becomes a blindman's buff
my dose of day.
Water turns to nectar in the throat
sleep is perfumed
profound.

You start beside me!
tripping over brambles
in some secret film.
You're a hot horse, lady
but all skin and skull
I cannot be within.

By plugging in and switching on
we've called a curfew
and mainline TV.
The modern man
takes his bath.
The water runs

the last lone cow shit
patters applause.
His dead head swings
like a bell full of blood.
The TV chatters on.

## Haircut

Arch back for fingers
strong as a wrestler
breathe the cup of her underarm.
Put the lights out, my masseur
be professional.

She's mine from the neck down
nails scoring the nape
belly, a clumsy child
pressing my shoulder.
I clench for maximum pressure

open a vein of love
to her cigarette skin
her tried and tested hair
straining to remain
a customer

talking to a stranger
full-face of a newscaster
a hand on my neck
a sudden breath
in my ear.

## Walnut

A brain in a sparrow skull.
Part of its two clam lips
inside, two hemispheres interlinked
a dry and fragile soul.
It takes surgical skill
to get one out whole.

My dad (who died) could
and once spied in a M.O.D. wood
green nuts, unripe for picking
but right for pickling.
I crawled, conscripted, under barbed wire
for those soft shells, for his desire
to create those shrunk black heads
loved by all of us (we said).

Hard skull or pickled soft
the walnut comes out every Christmas
as we pick over his long absence
on sofas, buggered with brandy.
We felt the cracks in his shell
probed gently but never really delved.

He always kept his kernel to himself.

## Red Snapper

I invited her for dinner
hoping to touch her
buying a fresh Red Snapper
to impress her
so I could press against her.
(*'Watch the dorsal spine'*, the sod had said).

At home it grew enormous in the sink.
I gutted it like a man
scraped off a thousand cellophane scales
then the dorsal spine (a tapering cartilage cocktail stick)
sunk deep into the hinge
of my finger
and snapped off.

I should have bought a joint of meat
but she was magnificent
for a pescetarian.

As it was
I liked her small red strapless dress
she disliked my large red snapless fish
and squealed when she saw the
        cooked cataract eye
        open mouth
        burnt tail and fin (minus spine).

I lost appetite.
One fingered, I started an invasion anyway
but she wouldn't let me touch the moist white meat
she only liked fillets
she felt sorry for it
but not for me.

I felt sorry for me
my finger throbbing and stiff with pain.
Nothing else throbbed all evening.
I bid her goodnight

left handed.

Two years later
sitting under an anglepoise I felt a small sharp prick.
I took a pair of pliers
and like a cowboy pulling a Cherokee arrow
tore the Snapper spine straight out
perfectly preserved, cartilage white, in a blob of blood.
I passed a moment in sweat and shock
at my bravery.

Now
whenever I finger my finger
I feel the pain
of that wasted Red Snapper.

## Young Mother

On silver mornings
the young mother is beautiful
December's nip in her cheeks.

She delivers to school
then retraces frost footprints
to a terrace on thermostat heat.

A mug of coffee is a treat
in a kitchen becalmed of children.
She wipes work surfaces, writes a list

*tinsel, chestnuts, stem ginger...*

then to the shops to cluster
in the clubs of motherhood
for pavement talk.

She has the day as a gift
and hopes to do Christmas
not quite the way her mother did.

Don't smile or stare
at lips and cheeks so carelessly bare.
Don't you see, she'll only insist

*love is the last thing on her list.*

## National Trust Woman

A profile amongst the portraits
a sketch of living lips
no cracked or blackened varnish
just fine pencil lines
pastel thin
English

brassiere chalked under jumper
white leg of summer, a skirt
that drapes thigh, hip
the anatomy of a perfect sitter.
Like any portrait, she won't make the mistake
of glancing at the painter

finding men a bore
dodging amateur photographers
each man trying to make a score
by focussing his camera.
I too, try my little ego
by sketching this quick cameo

guessing that on a luxury estate
she's stuck in an acrylic portrait
never having the pluck or fate
to face the symmetry of her face
accepting a fat executive
as a fat cheque mate.

Now, at tea, her pale charisma
keeps me glancing past my wife's shoulder
talking art as if it mattered
but being just another voyeur
trying to say in my aesthetic way
I'm a painter, not a predator.

## Doctors and Stars

Half a life learning how to cut and sew
closing holes in hearts, opening birth's canal.
How they worshipped you, coming in their droves
you gave them everlasting hope
they gave you roses, this garden in Park Road

where you strike a match, pipe at the ready
hold its flame to the stars
(with their extravagant, wasteful energy)
knowing there is neither elixir nor evil
just luck, and its reversal:

Planets that turn barren waists to suns
begging for conception.
In the universe
there is so much space, gas, dust
too little earth warmed by stars.

Yet here, chance grew knowledge
delivered generations of doctors
cutting, stitching
giving a few more years (at best)
or prognosing fear, disease, death.

All, in turn, raked into the garden
having tasted the same sweet medicine:
The sun will always rise
the roses will live on.
Until, sucked into a black hole

the match itself burns out of fuel
and without audience, without fuss
Earth becomes a spoonful of the latest dust
all knowledge, time, medical science
(even God)
effortlessly lost.

## Breakdown

I am the breakdown, the poor sod
at the side of the road.
My city shoes press into a verge of mud
virgin as the moon
a thousand commuters queue
to pass me by.

I am a disease
something unpleasant at the side of the road
a carcass stinking in a stream
a bolder the flood can't wash down.
I am a haemorrhoid
threatening to burst.

Engine without symptom!
I am a fallen angel
dropped in the gusset of the road
whose drivers (clean as motel guests)
queue to rape without care or condom
clamber over my feathers like army ants.

No oil or wine
only two thousand eyes that cross
to the other side.

## Forgetting

Sky
buried sky as leaf fell on loam
weeks rotated in a drum
dull month mouthed dull month, dead fish on a shelf
shoved up one end
layered in dust.

Days
insects trapped in pages, leaves left out in the rain
fibre pulp and fishbone vein.
Last summer
clings like wet tissue
to the bone remains.

Time
dulls my head
that I could squeeze one fragrance
from this bland brain
tweezer out cells which clot and drain
but mildew stinks the old closet where the volumes lay.

No pages left
pulped apples from the press
one homogenous day.

## They

In the morning
the glass is cracked like lightning
the canvas slashed to pork crackling
Stanley's knifed again.
The door, dismayed at its damaged thighs
is open wide.
We follow the trail of bad breath
through a second-hand house.

Where the birthday bicycle leant
is now a wall
where the candlesticks stood
two dust stencils.
The housewife washing in the window
was a colour transparency
(we thought, a private film)
but two fans were waiting by the stage door.
Her underwear has been lightly fingered
in the drawer.

Now all suns are set
keys twisted, bolts slid
drawbridges lifted
each house left to its own devices
in no-man's-land.
There is no silence in silence
only the trip wire of insomnia
every footstep a hair-trigger
in the minefield of moonlight.

They are out there
waiting for the last lookout
to fall asleep.

## Allotments and Digestives

On Sunday morning we few old men
bend our kidneys against the cold
and gather shabby vegetables
tenderly clean earth from our spades
and the anaemic roots of leeks.
With bloodless hands we prune the gooseberries
light small fires of green twigs
watch the altars twist the smoke skywards.

This is our afterlife.
We have no eschatology
only cold hands close to death
and the camaraderie of our barrows and spades
whose wooden handles we'll grip into the grave.
Together we survived the war, together we'll end our days
messmates within these iron gates
compost, brandling and bindweed.

In January the leaves are mulch black
that is how we love them
frosted casts of worms and winter couch grass creeping like veins.
The black horse chestnuts wait without hope of spring
cold English worms pull their stalks into tepees
and eat feasts underground.
We will wait until the summer air is warm as tea and thick with cabbage stalk
then we'll throw in our hand.

Thus blessed
we leave when it's too dark to dare
dig another trench.
Our season is at an end.
We sit in 60 watt rooms
wait for meat, mash
brussel sprouts and tea
God
and digestives.

## Blood

O
u
t
of
your
forearm
drips a syrup
rich enough to lick
each blob bursts, skins
to a chocolate drop of red.
Pressure! Pressure! Pressure!
The old way said tight tourniquet
compassionate hands constrict
but now it is hands off
check your gloves
for nicks.

## Antimacassars

Antimacassars
preserving the future in the front room
things we keep nice, unworn, aside
a suit for weddings and funerals
mummified.

Covering the table to stop distress
keeping the best china for best
put it on the wine coaster
keep it nice
for a house clearance of the future.

When the future was a child's summer
not these years concertinaing
into black plastic bin liners
these clothes, dated and uncreased
napkins kept for guests, long deceased.

All these will be antiques, sold
with photographs of our dead family
auctioned off accidentally.
A young couple will gut the house
throw into a skip

the antimacassars
saying: life is too long
not to wear things out
life is too short
for antimacassars.

## Spearing a Fish

Clenching toes naked on the canoe prow
eyes tracking the fish cruising the green water
right arm cocked with the spear
heavy with iron
waiting for the canoe and fish
to fuse momentum
*WHIPLASH IT DOWN*
the instinct of the dead line
piercing the weighted grace
of that undulating tail.

Clenching teeth on a supermarket trolley
eyes tracking the meat cramming the display unit
right armed cocked at the wrist
heavy with hesitance
waiting for the trolley and meat
to fuse momentum
*WHIPLASH IT DOWN*
the impulse of a dead time
piercing the taut polythene
of that motionless meat.

## Motorway Daddy

*Dad*
*I couldn't care less*
*for your whisky breath*
*and some secretary's legs astride you.*
*You've gone too far*
*with your company car*
*you're too easy to hate*
*coming back past eight*
*don't expect me to wait*
*I couldn't care less*
*for you.*

Executive shirt tourniquets the showered
flesh of the neck
eyeballs cornered, contentious
hair a photo-fit wig
Daddy sits, a combed prop forward
reborn in his leather seat
sebaceous and shaven with self-love
the eager smile of the sycophant.
Success brings its reward, of course.
Under the hang of his polyester paunch
his legs are almost too weak to walk
but strong enough to squeeze
the accelerator of his corporate pride
with vestigial ease.
He fingers the switches with delight
and, as the first sweat seeps
the first heart valve bleeds
Daddy is on the road.

Armpits of fear.
All is panic and power
a hundred daddies sit preying in their cars
possessed
brains and nerves kneejerk with all the rest
arcade pilots
twitching for the kill.

Retribution and skill
prove no family man has lost his drive
to overtake, outpace all the rest
to achieve a living in this daily test
of fate upon the road.
Craniums craning
heads of wire necks
pop-up eyes on stalks
men in machines, flesh in thin tin gowns
hunt and hate
eighty-five m.p.h.
brothers of the road.

He closes his eyes
finds love in the droning tyres
but can't find a dream
as the motorway screams
D A D D Y
Jammed in a slip road with a small angel of death
he looks out on God's valley beside the road.
We're all in this ballistic hell
caught in the flow
of crushed car foil.
Shrapnel and skid marks
are our art
our final parting to the kids back home.

Back home
a present for his son under his arm
bought in the garage on the way home.
*I'm in my bedroom with my headphones on*
*I've got my homework to do.*
Daddy remembers the good times
drinks his whisky all alone
shares some camaraderie with his cell phone
then steals into his son's bedroom
for a glimpse of the face of love
he used to know.

## Drunk at Christmas

A young drunk in town
swears he's Jesus Christ
and begs for change.
I lie to him
and lie run over on the carpet
a dry-eyed drunk driver
fallen from the Christmas tree
tinselled and titivated by TV.

We have conversed with neighbours
about the size of mortgages and buggies
the parents-in-law
about cats and aperitifs
people at a party
about hardware and management information.
Everyone is so pleasant.

Now the TV's gone cold.
I lie legless, crashed on the carpet
caught in the eternal heaven of Christmas
only these veins pulsing
with passing time.
Cold turkey in the manger
waiting for snow
from a whirlpool sky.

## Man the Alchemist

He stands erect
tripods his legs
two crutches
spreads his load
fans his hand
hides peeping Tom
his eyes reverencing
the tiles below.

A jerk of skin
the purple head so bold and rude
protrudes
a lipless porpoise smile of doubt
the sullen pout
of a blind old mole.

The accompanying vein
and goitred skin, a delicate thing
a petal purse of oil stones
brought to light, albino white
lettuce thin.

The barometer trips
the fluid climbs and slips
its pipe
rides the lazy rainbow
a steaming, arching, yellow
flight
a chemical checklist
a scented blessing.
Man the honest
alchemist

wags his wand
steps off his podium.
Man the alchemist
has created gold.

## Infant School

The school draws mothers across the moor
moaned by winds and grey winter air
they walk in ones and twos
winter ewes
on pin legs that pull them up unmarked paths
to the fold.

Outside the classroom
each mother waits to greet her lamb
side by side, the flock divides
according to class and clan.
Ewe eyes ewe
sheepishly.

The pen opens
out run the lambs on wobbly legs
each bleats to his mother's breast
who licks and sniffs her treasure.
Now all are together
for every mother
loves her lamb the best.

## Surgery

She's in the pilot's hands again
on the hospital bed
in her christening gown
listening down the intercom
smug words from the smug surgeon.
The anaesthetist injects gentle thrust
I keep my fingers
crossed
and the plane takes off.

The stewardess is making bedside jokes
will this cigar tube really float?
Hang onto the thin rope
my love
as you leave the juddering ground.
I'll know, when I hear the phone
to buckle my seatbelt up at home.

God urged and schemed
lured from the apes
some new dreams.
Now we can fly in terror
now we can hit the ground.

## Lord of All Hopefulness

We are krill
and float in our millions
a seething phosphorescence.
The whale slides an endless tunnel of love
a black-bellied guzzler, she swallows stars by the ton.
We spot her open gape
a twist of grin, a grid of teeth
generations are sieved
from the massage of the sea.
We have bobbed in the tides without hope
for we are scum
and skid in shambles across earth's surface
our veins barely hold enough phlegm
to flush hearts
flickering under our spectral skins.
We are spectacled, powdery
peeling, ordinary
ill with dislocation
we scurry in sea beds
but cannot leave the ocean.
We are confounded, God
our prawn chests are wheezing a hymn of salvation
please gulp us down.

As flies
we teem in our millions
temporary visitors for a season
we cluster on cut flowers in stained glass windows
stretch out necks for nectar
tongue the bones
folded under pews in prayer.
There is hope in the church's stone groynes
the perpendicular crosses and marble memorials
are confident of something.
Our minister is a lifesaving surgeon
he operates in full colour sermons
dispenses medals to all his congregation
'Never say die'

and kiss his hairy hands for salvation.
Keep your fingers crossed
he is an honest salesman.

As woodlice
we bury our dead in millions
under tombs
damp in prayers of peat and putrefaction.
We bow our heads under armoured eyelids
we have frugal constitutions
a composite soul sprinkled amongst millions
we chant prayers in unison
curl tight into balls
our thumbs in our mouths
our hands guard our genitals.
We kneel in prayer
stare
at the minister's immaculate, military shoes.
All will be crisp and neat
in the next world.

Thus, orphaned in our millions
we lie head to toe in hospital corridors
shedding our fragile wings.
The minister's hands are outstretched
to prolapsed tongues
say 'Aaaa...men'
then hang onto the altar rails.
There is some salvation, something to revere
in a silver chalice
there's no malice here
just a firm palm ironing
doubt from the skull
everyone needs a daddy somewhere
a knee to sit on, when you're tired and testy
a hand on your forehead
when you're twitching into a nightmare.
But the wafer sticks
not a drip of red reaches the outstretched lips
the wine circles the cup

like a broken heart valve
there's seldom enough to go around

for we are krill.
We sway the seas
we crawl the lawns
we swarm in hope
Lord
of all.

## Action Replay

After
I've popped off
get the AKAI video down from the loft
find an old box marked
'Family 91'.
Switch on.

This tape
has lain untouched in the attic
now the antique machine spits electrostatic
as the screen
reveals a garden scene.
Your children are laughing hysterically
at a figure they find derisory.
The young man in tasteless swimming trunks
is me

holding your hand, jumping off the wall
time and time again
your toddler legs splay
in action replay
on the moist summer lawn.
All is sun and shade
conifers stripe the grass
your sister splashes, baby arms
crazily conducting in the paddling pool.
Watch! A shadow falls across the path!
That is the lovely young wife
I used to have.

I know this sequence off by heart
your hot sticky hand
your dad playing the part.
Remember that kiss?
I was flesh and bone
not this will-o'-the-wisp
on a vintage video.

## The Painting

Now the room is warm
walls distant as sand dunes
the flat skin of a drum
taut, translucent.
We have made a division
we have made a partition
we have a room.

The painting
too easily overlooked in its frame
breaks its vow
flicks a phlegm of colour
takes its inaugural bow.
Inaudible itself, it
speaks to the sentient room.

A barn, a fence, a field
of corn
distant birds thin as hairgrips
fly with no legs
white clouds steam from the frame.
The artist looked up, then down
a thin track of flattened grass
beaten brown
barn to field
field to farm.

Through the window the cars
guard their road
aeroplanes expose
silver waistcoats
(they do not fly but float
like bombs, drop down a corridor).

Car hunts car.
The window clears its throat
a frame of tearing tyres
and nasal turbine whine

a tank of violent light
gouging the eyesight.

The painting
festooned in an age of seasoned light
lifts broken leaves to a perfect sky
trembles from the past.
The window drops its lid
shuts off its light
admits it is
blind.

## Conkers

A barrow of conkers dumped by the fence
is now a bonsai forest
of palm trees stretching stem by stem
their five-leaved hands
heckling for space.

Conkers know well the time
to swell, split, send out stiff tongue
to probe the land chance has them lie
in a bed of loam
or at the bottom of the pile.

One or two stretch with zest
head and shoulders above the rest
those flaunted fronds are in the know
they who grow fastest
shade those below

whose shrunk and twisted limbs
cram like beansprouts
claw stone
or, sliced by the guillotine of the spade
abort and rot

for the few to make secure
by sinking roots through their brothers' manure.
This is the conker's small glee
with a cannibal's conscience
they sharpen their teeth

and eating their fill in princely style
they roll, providentially
to the top of the pile.

## Clandestine

Not two
but four of us, or more
would meet ('I can be very discreet')
walk the glass corridor
sit, trainee divorcees
feeling for the heat (of your thigh)
'Clandestine', I say, you smile with your teeth
post sentries in cafes and on the streets
warning from the lid of your eye.

Not two
but five of us, or more
would meet
(touch hands, nudge knees, 'Sit by me please')
finding a friend's flat near and neat (it has no memories)
feeling for your hair and neck between the trees
'No one knows
you're here', you say
'Clandestine', but hoping the day
will break
the Christmas diners drift away
leaving
not two
but you and me.

## Sunlight in Salisbury

Who plumbed in these English months
like a row of gargoyles, leaking, spluttering
leaving our gardens infertile
drab as sullen women
leaning on their mops.

Jaundiced, we peer under sidelights
stay inside
taste the garish palettes of TV.
Tanned celebrities garnish
the murk of our luckless lives.

We drive in culverts
between verges airbrushed
with the scum of passing cars.
The winter wraps her skirts
of wet plaster.

We walk Salisbury Close
the giant cathedral cardboard, upright
but still pressing its mass into the grass.
Then the sun glimpses a gap
and like the lungs of a blue baby

our capillaries flush with pink new blood.

The houses suck light
through roots permanent as the pigments of earth.
We are artists reborn and daub
brush after brush of colour
splattering the brick, stone and lawn.

We breath this palette.
Slate bequeaths us lichen in bright yellows
moss fluoresces on pebbles
a thousand stones give up the light
quarried from their bones.

All eras have coalesced
for this moment of collage
this planting of houses with green fingers.
We have propagated a mirage
of earth itself.

Those who merely glanced through office windows
return home in the evening
their colours weaker
their sunshine theoretical
watered down.

But we have received our incubation
we have received intensive care from the sun.

## Kites

Pressing the wind
gauze-thin
cotton coloured hills
suspended in spills
of disbelief.
Two-finger tested
they billow the blue
full as spinnakers

or sewn in triangular seams
that cleave from clavicle
roll in gait, joggling
jabbing, beckoning
palms to cup
the thrust of the wind.

Baboons moon bare bums
so man barred his brawn
his valve undone, slavering
as she-apes jogged the plain
their kites dancing.
Man's lot, forever ogling
probing
at kites
jellying the wind.

## You Know You'll Fail the Test

When you wake up in sweat
with the damp blanket of death
and the sash window fails to move
and you lie with your flesh
and your flab on the bed
and you hope the hoses
don't split in your head
and there's no cell in your lung
mutated or dead
or a lump in your gut
or a clot in your neck.
You've a crack in your back
from the ditch of the bed
and you wonder how *they*
faced up to the end
such a private event
everything ending in bed
what they thought
what they said
and you know
in the end
you'll fail to impress
you know in the end
you'll fail the test
you know
in the end
you'll fail.

## Do-It-Yourself

'You fucking bloody wanker!'
he roared
and roared off in his car
(red and sexy
of course).
So I sat in my family car
(consumer plastic and flush-fit glass)
outside the Do-It-Yourself store
(architect green with garden-centre grass).
Me in my everyday car
(practical and very discreet)
and thought about taking his advice
and not wanking for at least a week.

All men wank
but I would save my semen in its own soft fridge
for him.

Or I could save it for her
faded tan body
and French plaited hair.
I could refrain from do-it-yourself
put the electric drill back on the shelf
and not wank for a week.
Build up to some Polyfilla hell
tour 'Wallpapers' and 'Fixings' for a treat.
She could present her electrical beauty aids
on full heat
until the wallpaper steams
peels off.

> Whimper thin harem knickers
> cushions of warm female ham
> drifting silk, lace stocking hold-ups
> thin suspenders sellotaped on thighs
> brassieres broken-backed on Bo-Peep breasts.
> All M and S best, of course.

In a state of mock undress
with feigned surprise I'd find her on the bed
taste the onion soup on her breath
anticipating a frenzy of middle-aged sex
where I would perform like a builder in jeans
the act
of hammer-drilling and rawl-plugging my dreams.

So all men must ask
whether to save their sperm for her best days
or spill it away
in their own hormonal way
on red cars and do-it-yourself.

## Road Improvement

They have improved the road, father.
Where once it kinked like a varicose vein
it's now stretched and slick
commuter fit.

My car hums
its tyres bear praise, its bumpers sing
*Oh Tipp-Ex lines, almighty signs*
*immaculate bitumen.*

But you are lost in the fast and clean.
On the Ordnance Survey's embroidered plan
let me draw you a line
with a sweep of my hand.

Thick and red.

Streaking out homes, the pub, that tricky left turn.
For father, we fly over.
Only by drones will we learn
where we are and where we've come

where our old bridge has gone.
The lane we pedalled, the ups and downs
the potholes
all ironed out.

## The Evil T

There, the evil T
his black widescreen
red eye of deceit.
Stand by

for blabber.
Eight million (or sixteen)
eyes he'll will to screen
thread on a skewer

of his tainted light.
This is the Plutonian plague
for adult or child.
Dalek

he fires a kind of colour
at a weak world
preserving forever
without flavour.

When I was a kid, he kidnapped
when I was a man, he manacled
when I was old, he sold
my last boxed soul.

The choice is
a real world
or effortless submission
to his remote control.

## Garden Shed

Like so many dads, you died
leaving a pipe and a photograph
a set of tools, ready for use
sharpened in a box.

The things you made do not dismantle
every cut a perfect right angle
your forearm twisted with gristle and metal
torque
and your will was done.

Wood was disciplined by your eye
and I
by your hand, not honouring
the sign that spelt: KEEP OFF THE GRASS
jointed, sanded and screwed
countersunk and Cascamite glued.

You had a bellyful
of me and my nails.

You built it round the back
in days of feet and inches
bradawl, sawdust and brass screws
strewn across the grass.
Three by three PAR
(too good by far, for a shed)
mortised, dowelled and clad
in inch thick planks
tongue and grooved by hand.

You never bought off the shelf.

A daydream from the house
a boy may kneel, a disciple
feeding off the shed's dry smell.
A child amongst the cloches

may learn the spiders' secret nests
smudge vermillion mites on flowerpots
and execute an aphid's
feeble steps

sitting out the last few days of Lent
the beginning of the garden of absence.

## Guinea Pigs

Two sisters caged
nose to tail.
They made their decision
touched
and found comfort.
They licked and loved

never knowing a male's
meaty thrusts
only the fur of each other's belly.
Hold them vertical
check their organs
are identical

feel the trembling in their
untried thighs, testy eyes.
They fear discovery.
Their parents' dismay
at a love nest without babies
in the neat pressed hay.

## Papier-mâché

We tore up the paper
built hills, valleys, cliffs
a cave
mashed by hand
a wet landscape of newsland.

Ten layers of yesterday
pasted, smoothed
the crust hardening
exposing
half-digested news.

Now it's thick as plaster
we skin over the top layer
obliterate every scoop
with plain
white paper.

We bury a thousand dramas
and the papier-mâché of today
becomes
the landfill
of the future.

## Chicken

The chicken crouches like a stone
glances up.
Well grown, you old muscle of loam
I reassure
pull yellow feathers from the bird.

There's a girl in our office with skin like this
granular, pale, cold putty to the probe.
We can't electrify you back to life
my frozen girl.

Pressed flesh flexes
heart creeps upon board; muscle
pinched in fingers winces
arches up to the knife like a cat
pink sliced
in sleeping slugs lies cold.
Wings hinge, held up as limbs
rasped raw
splinters barb the baggy skin.
They are sad lost flippers.

Outside, my girl
you exercised hard, flapped bone and skin
but now I can't distinguish flesh
from breast, breast
from my squeezing.
I lick your sternum dry
take hold of your legs
pop your cartilage knees.
White pegs and legs
part in modest rigor mortis.

My hand screws up its face.
What cold mysteries
aubergine hard bulbs of vein and blue
swim beneath this skin?

She swallows hard and gulps me whole
self-satisfied, winks her parson's nose
her neck unrolls, she legless lies
the blood is spunk, the bird is cold
the offal's in the bin.

## Filling

Intimate, asexual
his fingers peel my lips
eyes focusing below my horizon
into a canyon.
He picks the jawbone

robot hands circumnavigating
vivisecting
steel cranes preying
angle-poised against
the twin sunrise

on a planet
where a skull is unearthed
teeth weathered to a row of metal plugs.
The jawbone gapes
released from its ache of gristle

from which he withdraws
his slow-motion needle, drilling
filling with foreign metal.
Shot that will drop from a rotten pheasant
some time after burial.

## Saturday Floodgates

Washed from a side street
in a gorge of gorgons
a multi-lane swim
a swerve, a belch, a chute

of sociology, a lust
of self-selection, all emblem.
Bone heads bob the flow
Brueghel's corpses

snag on cash dispensers.
Hair cut in slogans, water-logged
oafs swim in rows
girls with heads of froth

wobble every staccato heel
all fist and lip, chest deep
they bully between boulders
eddy, gold-fishing windows.

Weak swimmers, pushed from kerb
tread water in shop doorways
wait to be washed down tributaries
to old villages, seaside towns

knocked down
put out to drown
by the Tetris estates
the Saturday floodgates.

## Moment

The sky tight with grey and cloud.
I, horizontal
in bed
felled from the ground.
Outside in the street
lilting movements, pavements of oil
people, strangely triangular
propped up with legs
pass into fog, breath
and watery reflections.

Their trunks pass my window
vertical
taking steps, span
silver gutters
and a long, long wall of silence.

In the dreaming morning dismay
in the interior of my room
is a thought and a weak yellow light.
A thought so delicate, perilous
a single atom broken loose
a rare seed upon the wind
a moment of truth.

The thought is:
I, horizontal
the people, vertical.
Somehow forever. A thin thing hovers.
I knew it once before.
I knew
before thought had flaunted
distorted
a truth I had once learnt anew.

I, horizontal
the people, vertical.

Then the closed eye with nothing on it
looked up to clouds, rain
film of glass.
The day, the morning
lay flat.
Just people
walking by.

## Three Schoolmasters

*Georgie Porgie pudding and pie*
*Kissed the girls and made them cry*
*When the boys came out to play*
*Georgie Porgie ran away.*

### ONE

This man's a flesh heap
a Guy Fawkes stuffed with sausage and meat
a crate of ribs, Brontosaurus thighs
webbed reptilian eyes.

A frog squats on his nose.
Muscles swim side by side, submarine in fat.
He sports his chest like an oak wardrobe.
'We are men, we are hamstring and thigh!'

He loves to sweat and scents
when the boys come out to play
joins in, scrums with all the best
the 'Boys' Own' sex of play.

He loves the big boys
apes in schoolboy clothes
testes ripe as plums
the all-male loincloth bulge.

A communion of flesh
showers and perfumed buttock soap.
We are the big boys
men in schoolboy clothes.

## TWO

This man is chiselled cold
a Bakelite face, wire frame nose
saline skin reinforced
with violent canine rules.

Hair a plastic kit – photocopy thin
a neat militaristic chin
safety-pin lips, trousers zipped
crisp from groin to toe.

He loves cadets, mocks them erect
loves the little boys all in a row
and when the boys come out to play
he teaches them how to touch their toes.

He likes clean boys, pale and meek
fresh underclothes, hygienic sheets.
With the pups he plays the role of runt
the little boys queue to nip his throat.

The prepubescent tearful tease
the weight of the boy's hot, sweetened feet
he smacks their ever-so-naughty bums
presses his palm against their cheeks.

## THREE

This man takes his delicate step
calf leather shoes and pastel leg
balance is frivolous – the body's been bled
he's just a manikin on a wilted thread.

Sweet boy, sweet life, sweet kissless lips!
I feel our lives are a grand gimmick.
The intrigues! Men, fascinating men!
The curtain drops, the show is at an end

but when the boys come out to play
he resembles a dancer, recreates a play
of dreams celestial, a glittering hearth
dives naked into a pool of silken scarves.

Stroke me, stroke me, wrap me in hands!
I wear the scars of shaving, cursèd man!
The boys are soft with beautiful chins
shave me, save me, show me your sins!

A kiss from the dancer
love bite on the neck
a closet disaster
the boy's bedroom wrecked.

## Perfect Lovers

When you steal into your children's room
find them asleep inside their dreams
unplugged hands
breathing
like life support machines
you know there's no heaven or hell
just the love and the preaching of these
perfect lovers.

## Mother and Daughter

Seeing you two together, side by side
(full mane on one, the other rinse-dyed)
the virgin blush on your daughter's skin
is now too wholesome for your face of sin.

Egg after egg you shed and bled
sun, smoke, late nights to bed
(identikit eyes, Madame Tussaud nose)
as love grows older, I hope love grows

to cover the cracks, fill with makeup
the damage I'll do as your elixir dries up.
For no 'CAMAY' soap will screen-test you
your granny skull is pressing through.

## The Poggy

There it was
stuck to my manuscript.

Programmed to investigate, classify
my finger extended to analyze.
Fluff? Some form of soot?

No
still sticky
uncooked.

As first you denied
blamed the children
(but they were out
this poggy is fresh as dough).

Then your silent shoulders fell
condemned.
You'd picked, flicked for the fireplace
but, adhering to the fingertip
as poggies do
the trajectory of the projectile
was unpredictable.

Out of your nose came a poisoned poggy.
Out of your chattering hair, excited earrings
came this miniature demon.

There were others:
A Leonidas praline light-fingered from the fridge
various unconfessed farts.

But now we know for sure
we all do our delving in the dark
many a poggy is jettisoned
deception is everybody's art.

**Transit**

The business is transit.
A family firm, local as a snail
who undertake to pay the rent
from the ventless front room
where we wait
a family tree, newly pruned
on our first flight from home.

The box is the prize exhibit
cordoned off from unholy hands
the wood-effect panels, stick-on handles
part of an instalment plan.
It's got to be a DIY joke
which bits are unscrewed and recycled
and which bits go up in smoke?

The father and son are a comedy duo
trick handshakes limp as gloves
no laughs, only mourning suits
that fly out dead flesh and blood.
Charters leave every half hour
the cargo is safely stowed
just as the party's warming up
it's time for us to go.

We bend into the stiffened cab
the doors are firmly closed
the cortege selects a gear
appropriate to the payload.
We taxi past shoppers
strangely popular.
Diplomats for a day
in our lead limo.

With faces too anguished to talk
they check-in our holy load
it's heavy work shifting baggage
though she's only skin and bone.

Go on, drop it on the carousel, lads
it's just another terminal
in this busy aerodrome.

Finally it departs
like a suitcase at Heathrow.
Bournemouth keeps the business going
*DEPARTURES ONLY*
no flights home.

## Surf

We are out with the big guns.
Tanks
rolling off a giant production line.
We scan the rows of green steel.
Inhaling, they bulldoze moats
rear up like grizzlies
wheel to wheel, full throttle
spitting machine gun froth
from high turrets.

Wait
until their glistening bellies
overhang for the kill
see the curve of their claws
then ride, slide the thin armour
run before the wheels
the thrill
of slipping those snapping teeth

as they slap thighs
hitch kick.
We jack out
or get dumped in their tracks
snatched under
churned
minced in their gears
caught in a conveyor.

Spent
we glide from the battlefield
into the safety of the beach.
The scenery is coloured
3D
the echo
of the big guns
lost out to sea.

## Woman, 45

The past
saw you rise from the snare of child care
and organize yourself
lovers in bed-pressed clothes.
Lovers in letters
hidden in crevices
dusted on dry pine shelves
filed in drawers under
underwear
where *he* wouldn't dare
delve.
Numbers, days, caresses
slipped in diaries in folds.
But still *his* lust, *his* breath, *his* animal hair
and your body taking off its clothes
your body taking off its clothes.

The past
saw you welcome friends like old friends
to your home
your beautifully distressed Georgian home.
Living alone in grand living rooms
and driving your children below.
Collecting, shopping
arranging your hair
and your sensible sensual clothes.
Your husband suspecting
suspenders expecting
as you position your thighs just so.

The present
sees a new man late
to your lineage of lovers.
Lovers can't join your candle-lit suppers
so he showers and dances alone.
He's only just in your diaries
I suppose
but it's still for *him*

you buy those flimsy things
and position your hips just so.

The present
sees a heavier husband on the bed
and you having difficulty
finding your breath
as you position yourself below
*his* belly, *his* beer, *his* buttocks and bones
you organize yourself well, I suppose.
Friends
lunches
ironing and lovers
as you position your breasts just so.

The present
watches you watch
the lease upon your face grow old.
You're beautiful with age
soft buttocks and bones
but you start stealing your daughter's clothes.
Your new hair is a shock to your skin and your nose
as you position your lips just so.

The present
sees you still blessed with a body
the female fat of a body
that hugs those delicious clothes.
Whilst *his* success brings in faces
takes you to places
where he wouldn't dare delve.
But new love that found you
sadly
passing your best
can be breakneck and desperately bold
and your freckled back and unsure lips
your vascular thighs and swaying hips
still tilt and tip the soul.

So when you're down and out

and the night is black
*his* stubble on you back
and your breasts are in the cold
please forget
to position
yourself
so.

## Scan Man

The women sit, palms on their footballs
five fingertip stethoscopes listening to their domes.
They have forgotten the genesis
sex was last year's clothes
now it's cardigans and frocks
inward smiles
that focus down through surgical gowns to the puffballs inside.
They hope for a photograph to take into work.

Some read magazines
for magic has left these wombs
grown up, gone to school.
They refuse all good news
ask to be flushed, bled, scored
all polyps removed.
The posters of plump babies
are stealthily ignored.

He arrives
knows every shade of red and rouge
every expression from crotch to navel
every face, deflated or ballooned.
The hands of the faith healer and part-time plumber
knows when to cut and what to sever
it's all on TV, twisted from your view.
He can knot or untie you

for this is the hallowed ground
where blood turns to baby
or melts to mushed strawberry
grapes split
spit pips, seedlings lose their grip
and, in the thick of it
hormones weep.
From this warm centre all bombs burst.

One by one they leave
some with dreams

some with empty bottles
some with transplanted seeds.
He’s no cardiologist who mends broken hearts
he is the fishmonger, he slits from gill to cloaca
when he enters
life always departs.

## Dry Rot

Bite Australia – there is no rot
a dry thing scuttles for a dry rock
a lizard skin swaps electric leg for leg
parched thing
a tail, a fuse, a skinned snake head
a lipless smile, electrostatic twitch
his pot belly clots
cast bronze in the ditch.

The grass is artificial turf
a scurvy dust – transplant stuff
running barefoot on a deadman's crust
in bell bird
bell jar
heat.

This wasp's definitive goal
is to pick
alone
grain after grain of sand from a hole.
He does not think, he does not sweat
he moves Australia's desert alone
a shell, a death, a burnt-out egg
antenna, leg, antenna, leg
a timeless zone.

No decomposition – all is dry rot
a tree tears off its papyrus bark
white arm, fold of fat, a naked hole
an ivory leg of cemented bone.
Wax dipped leaves discontent in air's
oven
oven
breath.

The runner cuts his ditch
the link of jaw kicks heel to bone
a beat

a drone of feet and foot and dust and feet
black ants like people below.
The wasp
blitzed by those apocalyptic feet
splits, jackknifes, desiccates and leaks
sizzles on stone.

The runner ducks his hat
skewered, drips fat
runs on.

### Sydney Sunday

Rain drops like olives
a small gauge face haunts the widow frame
glass pleated with rivulets.
Then out he steps
ball and socket hips.
Heel to toe
heel to toe.

Old man in grey felt hat
spot, blot
then blotted black
head high with feint aplomb
shoes tug-boating against the spume.
Heel to toe
heel to toe.

Umbrella?
The bat wing rips
he grips the wire rib splints.
Shoes to the bilges!
Hands to the bone!
Heel to toe
heel to toe.

Water quoits his turn-ups
trees shout their branches
warning him, warning him:
Go home, old man, go home!
But he, old sailor, rides the foam.
Heel to toe
heel to toe.

He pauses
hinged on one coat-hanger toe
the kerb a subaquatic zone
and steps from sea to sun-kissed coast
a cartoon step of scurvy bone
and trouser capillarity.

Heel to toe
heel to toe.

One giant step to run aground
the green rimmed Terra Australis sand.
Unflagging
he inches on inland.
Heel to toe
heel to toe.

## Two Letters

Sleep's set sweet resin in my skull
fossil head pillowed in bed.
You come in, sit still
pale as a sheet.
Two letters:
One from a friend saying her husband is dead
one from friends on a beach.
David's dead, you said
sounding distant as the sea.

> Shoulder width tube through space
> Five floors he slid
> maybe someone, a nurse, glimpsed his face
> as he hid, head in hand
> plugging the bung of dread.
>
> His life was piquant
> a smile threaded from within
> his spine stiffened, green bone to stone
> he couldn't even bend to tie his own
> shoelaces – useless bloody things.

There's not much more to write, she writes
so we write, words like
human beings can't just die
shall we come over and see you sometime
we try
but give in.

To a strange tap I put strange lips.
Good morning!
Water slips, a lizard swims within
peristalsis is cold
comforting.

Remember sitting in the garden of 'The George'
cool grass between your toes?
He took his shirt off – a friendly stomach bulge

and a dog with body rigor mortised and old
drew close
dragging two legs like fence posts.

It tastes like sour white wine
waking up with the door slammed shut
the world indelibly bleached.

Out of the other letter breasts bulge
like sails.
Sand's gold grit sticks to wet bikini prints
salt on Margarita rims.
Vacuum thighs hang from bones
like hams
or spread
stranded as jellyfish on the beach.

The luxury of waking up in white sheets
waving brown toes.

> The sea is stuck in a plasma
> wedge on the sand.
> Black spiders surf the froth
> the sun cranks slowly up and across
> bodies crowd on
> each given a churchyard plot
> to lie, six foot by three, upon.
> Everyone splits their sides and oils their skin
> half pink, half burning
> modesty on the grill.

There's not much more to say, they write
except you must come up and see us sometime.
But sometimes
the long, long road of see-you-sometime
is permanently closed.

## Public School Common Room

Ducking arches of stone
dipping hatchets of light
I pinch through the airlock
seal the oven door
step into a mausoleum of air
effortlessly cold.

The room has been perfectly preserved during the night
a period piece set with
men in stone circles
newspapers, faint pencil sketches
sepia witnesses to the prints of the old school
waiting on the walls.
Plaques commemorating
the bald heads of the long dead
benefactors
dull with oxide film
and filth.

Boredom mesmerizes the air
hardwoods creak in silence
blunder into stone walls.
Headmaster heels in
in perfect tense
a perfect pedestrian
pedestal tall.
Small 'God warnings' are echoed by all
then snatched by the air before they fall
like goldfish gulping their own belches.

High above
bored thoughts crowd the skylights like grey balloons
a newspaper butterfly flaps
and settles on outstretched hands in a lap.
Secure in the knowledge
the boys are beaten
they chalk immaculate lines on the board

*for they shall inherit the earth*
those who are bored
while Sir stalks with a stick of chalk
never talks, only orders
SILENCE.

**Night Panic**

My body sack bolstered on the bed
thin logs beneath blankets
vestigial limbs
half swastika
on the sheet.

The window grey
crass
in black sieved air
silence fidgets like a whippet
gnats clench their teeth.

Bed floats in a sea of grey.

I
a single head
revolve slowly
a spider
on my thread.

Window
no longer anchors light
has no sense
but its grey lid is shut
tight on the world.

*Inside a cave in the wind*
*on earth's primed surface*
*paramecium gnaw*
*moss sniffs at rock*
*toads trombone*
*glass eyes skim*
*swamp*
*and scum.*
*New bubbles burst new water*
*under a slanting sun.*

Beside me in bed

a badger groan leaks from
the finger-hole in your sleeping lips.
I see the thin trail of a man across the world.
My innards scream
craving you, you
to help me with all this.
But all you can do
is cling monkey limbs
in tonight's primeval world.

**Drum n Bass Dubai Diary**

'This is my personal vision of Hell,'
you yell
staring out the trillionth floor
from our airlock balcony door.

'Personally, I like piles,' I say
pointing to the vast display
of piling machines, insecting space
beating out their drum n bass.

'They're planning more palaces to rise
from these deserts of concrete spikes.'
'Unfinished wastelands,' you cry.
'Yes, yes, but look at that blue sky.'

The hotel – a giant sheet of glass
dazzles us specimens on the fake grass
there's gilded villas we're meant to gawk
and griddled streets too hot to walk

so we take an icebox car inland
where chic cement hides desert sand
here Arabs sport NY baseball caps
and crazy rich Asians wear all the brands.

Hiding in dhotis, sunburn black
Indians squat down dirt side-tracks.
'Hopefully they're not too badly paid
those palm implants give 'em shade.'

Now we are diplomats in marble halls
where souks are pseudo shopping malls
the choice, they chant, is up to you
Jeremy Corbyn or Jimmy Choo?

The Burj Khalifa asks why it's born
and was bottle-fed testosterone
the pool's horizontal as the sea

and tiny planes fly in human fleas.

We cannot find anything distressed
lounge by the pool with all the rest
bronze and brazen sunbed hoarders
deftly dial-up cocktail orders.

You search for a surface, other than sand
that you want to touch with your pale hand
'Anything small and green,' you cry
'It's not your allotment, it's Dubai.'

Here the sun seems to bear a grudge
so we hide in our hotel, try not to judge
it's all got a bit too much
and the balcony handrail's too hot to touch.

## The Sims. It was our love of sausage dogs and black leather

super-sized breakfasts brought us together.
FYI – I weigh in at thirty, too fat to be flirty
she too carries full flesh contrary to Barbie
we walk Saucisson & Chorizo at night
dodge the derision of the Sims people's spite.

We write in the dark to avoid their mockery
MA Creative Writing? No, we sprinkle cheese in a factory
burp words like *turducken*, don't hide behind low-calorie
we are full-flavour, plump, fleshy and masterly
our T-shirts sweat big buckets of vocabulary.

Our bard bugles paid for our house and muddy drive
we gorge succulent sausages dripping fat and life
now we piss on the simulants who starve to stay alive
with their white-wall flats and anaemic thighs
pretentiously pausing between words      *to/survive.

We cook mountains of poetry, pile our plates high
pages tasting of wit, landscape, colour and life
how we pity the poet posing with one word per line
advertising herself on her internet shrine
copycat poems petrified of the capital i.

We write full-fat, deep-fried, wringing with molasses
words drunk with colour on a thousand drunken canvasses
we grab pots of life, splashing, laughing and farting
spill food on paintings, twisting, rolling, disembowelling
paint from planets of which the Sims know nothing.

Now we laugh as they walk their dry bones on leads
words split with microtomes on pages of conceit
magazines of meaningless monotony, anorexic lines
blank sheets of their one-leaf salad-choked lives
each poem a pick-n-mix of their flat white lies.

## Frome Auction

You stand, light-house for danger
but you give him a long leash
watch your son climb palings
fail, fall
learn mud.

There's a modesty to your eye
a couldn't-care-less-ness
dirt palms are good for the whole
worn hands
earthenware bowls for the soul.

Inside the auction, you finger second-hand whispers
dust, threads, hair trapped in hinges
brown cupboards, brown chairs, castoff clothes
salvage for your household
frugal hands will remould.

Your hair – a triumph of tribe over tradition
threaded, felted, knotted
leaves me besotted – a kind of primal smell
Kurdish kitchens, nappy-bucket bedrooms
embedded human pheromones.

Outside, you load your horse and cart
Bruegel art
your son wrapped in a backpack
a days of yore throwback.
you expertly rope the jumble on the back.

Caught in the traffic queue behind you
it has to be said, what is true?
You were a spectacle
we were awkward, respectable.
Our car condescendingly overtakes you.

## Purgation

All dogs are more equal, two paws equal four
tearful tails are indispensable, it's the yippee yappy roar

of hound dog, guardian, retriever, castrated mutt or spay
a million crossbred whiners, every mongrel wants its day.

Pet petulance? Bellicose bark? Whatever colour, breed or cur
purge your bowels all over the park, catwalk your selfie-bred fur.

Poor old Plato would have a fit, arse-sniffing is the new way
a million pooches' piss and shit, every whinging woof has its say.

Puppy pimple? Dalmatian spot? We're so much more than internet cogs
we demand shit in every shot and chat-show CBT for dogs.

Poor pooch – coat's been clipped? Then get yourself on lapdog TV
we're all dog-eat-dog addicts, it's all about bow-wow, all about me.

Votes for oysters and votes for dogs, a virtual Bertrand Russell brawl
you hound-humping demagogues have forced toxocariasis upon us all.

The pampered puppy in the PC window, costs a higher price every day
these dogs are not just for Christmas, they're barking never gonna go away.

**Delft Love**

Truth is indisputable, it's verifiable fact
so I should tell her the truth, no need for tact
straightforward, simple, a single book on the shelf
she's a loony Hume bundle, *she only talks about herself.*

To clarify, she is a junctionless autobahn
she drives up it one way, going on and on and on
an automatic gearbox, unbroken white-line words
lips undulating like fat buttocks squeezing turds

an endless lung blast of self-masticated self-worth
a vomitus of barely munched thoughts in reverse
her mouth disgorges helpless word after word
her eyes rotate 180 degrees to her preferred

self-service autobiography, a sort of identity concentricity
an empty lane carriageway of her anthropocentricity
a self-absorbed conveyor-belt of infinite capacity
a sodden, dripping sponge of syrupy self-gluttony.

At dinner, she heads the table, a bowerbird bullfrog
and, overlooking us trinkets, works up a drunken monologue.
I don't think it's mental health or just flypaper narcissism
it's introspection without grace, a kind of dinner party fascism

so I say, 'Don't you realise *you're loony, you only talk about yourself*
you're a *loony lunar loner, not interested in anyone else.'*
She suspends her solipsism, looks down at the blue Delft
'You've been to the moon, I've been to the *blue moon* myself.'

## Pastéis de Nata

No carrot sticks here, no amuse-bouche
just walrus-wide pastry, extra calorie food
full cream custard, a double-dome bum
never a drumstick, always a bass drum
plus-size, bus-size, bountifully bariatric
every part superfluous, acres of fabric

brontosaurus skin of fresh white bread
a bust bigger than a bicephalous bolster bed
engorged arms flustering at her side
she panic sits, creates a flesh landslide
the chair cringes under her freshly logged weight
a full moon face in a carbohydrate landscape.

This modern tribe, a new standardised norm
a shopping mall XXXL, sit-in-café lifeform
militantly big, fat-shaming ain't their thing
they're proud, plenteous, bon viveur-ing
but as she rises, balancing her mammary glands
her eyes lash me with a *'I have rights'* whiphand

which declares she's fit and should fit right in
yet in practice she can't fit into anything
couldn't risk a bike, a bus, train or plane
she'll never see the view from a zip wire again
she thinks I'm judging her persona non grata
but I'm loving every curve of her pastéis de nata.

## Turl Street Truck Oxford

A thousand thick students me me me talking talking
intelligent my arse, they're stood right behind, yakking yakking
stuck-up students me me me posing
hyperactive tongues chit-chatting chin-wagging
stood right in the way of my 4-axle beeping beeping
I'm inching back hoping, inching back hoping
back-up beeper beeping, warning warning
I'm heavy metal death, death metal reversing
tight-titted on Market Street's 40-point turning
yeah, look down on me, I'm a prick for diagonal driving
mirror's a millimetre away from your thick head thumping
nosing Jesus College, tyre-wall kerb scraping clutch burning
you must know you're plumb in the way, standing jawing
bikes bombing out Brasenose Lane, legs peddling, careering
no common-sense or helmet, gap swerving wobbling
girl's a hairbreadth from annihilation, total unthinking
it's tighter than a camel's arse in a sandstorm howling
no one gives a bollock about distributing delivering
Oi toff tits, you even awake? me me me schmoozing
it's food for your effing market, your effing eating and drinking
I'm right rammed-in now, half-inching, half-inching
their head's still in the clouds, socialising gossiping
any normal bloke would wave directions to me backing
look out tossers, this is serious weight moving
one slip of my foot and you're dog meat haemorrhaging
blow the horn, wake the buggers up, honking honking
they're stood there deliberate, defiantly confronting
these so-called brainbox b-leaders ain't got no learning
the trouble is their whole kind thinks
talking is working.

## Moving Story

Her grandad died, blown to smithereens on the beaches of Normandy
her twin babies burst two months prematurely
she found love on a bikini-island opportunity
cried on screen, leaking silicon coyly
we have tears, we have a moving story

her mental health nose-dived, dusted with Whitehall austerity
she crowdfunded a memorial for her dead pet's posterity
fought cyber-bullies to gain star-studded popularity
laughed 'til she cried, a tear-jerking celebrity
we have tears, we have a moving story

she gripped a stranger's hand as a jet plunged to infinity
her pain will be felt by Facebook friends for an eternity
lost for words, she spoke about unspeakable cruelty
bit the dust unfairly at a suntan-fuelled party
we have tears, we have a moving story

the doctors didn't do nuffin, she alone fought cancer bravely
never threw in the towel, sprayed positivity on chemically
started a new charity for A-list facelift memory
selflessly took selfie after selfie
we have tears, we have a moving story

she swapped gender without her parents' authority
crashed her white Audi whilst texting courageously
so full of life, campaigned for hen-party diversity
slid to her grave on a mountain's unguarded gravity
we have tears, we have a moving story.

## 2020 Flood

At first they just oozed
rancorous, discourteous as drains
then they flooded
covering the colossi with sludge
carved stone, porticos, windows, decoration
the carvings, mouldings, drawings
(engineer doctor philosopher scientist musician)
all beauty and precision
sodden and instantly derelict.

The cowering hinges and rotten frames
the smashed light let in more of their flood.
'Whoosh,' they say. 'Whoosh!' throwing a hand
over their heads in mock comedy.
They bang their bastard drums
spitting slogans, a million dumdum raves
shouting cursing larfing through the streets at night
gobby, guttural, carping, craving
cocky as drug dealers, streetwise as mud.

They are out there now
telling you shut up
or they will set their thick dogs on you
smash your dovetails
transport you to the fields.

Keep to your house. Hope to die before they bring in
their tub-thumping oaths.
Their dark age.

No ark
just Morlocks
grinning.

## Injustice

He is a mild-mannered Mohican
wears T-shirts with cherry-picked slogans
his spouse colours her hair mellow yellow
*'you know her – vegan dogs, plays the cello'*
for daily dyspepsia, he gobbles the Guardian
wrapped against chill in a broadminded cardigan

spectating injustice is his life's motivation
from his cosy bedroom workstation
wouldn't use an airline if you paid him
cycles everywhere to decry transportation
in truth, he's a little nervy of exotic places
glamorous ladies, working men's faces

he reads column after column of affronted lesbians
sex-trafficking, austerity, poisoned pedestrians
bee killers, migrants, fat cat capitalists
supermarket plastics and fracking fascists
each tale feeds his John Lennon spectacles
with *'someone ought to do something'* hypotheticals

boasts he once cycled all around Scotland
*'with a Green government there'd be no problems!'*
a peculiar type of self-absorbed humanism
a wicker-man worshipper of George Monbiot-ism.
One day biking to buy his local farm vegetables
the farm truck flattens him and his spectacles.

## Breach

This is no place for millionaires and snowflakes
tuck yerself back in yer Teslas with yer gluten-free cakes
here ya gotta wring yer own sodden socks, lift yer own soddin feet
there's no waiters to love ya, no lacto-veggie matsutake to eat
it's brutal not Bruton – think mud, flood, barbed wire and muck
the rain is shitting 18-wheeler 40-tonne trucks
no Frostrup At the Chapel, no Le Chameau brand boots
just bullyboy buses blood-hounding the Hinkley Point route.

This is not rain you can duck with umbrellas and Ubers
it drenches sand sea silt sludge, all sods and sewers
this is the saturate of Somerset, an estuary empty of landscape
a drain to drown newcomers, a leech mother who eviscerates
lift yer own weight through quagmire, saltmarsh, swamp and mud
there's no prize at the end, no cafés, bijou Bath-stone pub
it's a two-mile foot-slog of shape-shifting shit and sediment
not for you city weekenders with yer white trainer arrogance.

Just plant yer frigging feet 'til you get to the tidal froth
there's no countryside to speak of, just a bucketing backcloth
the bruised breach of the Parrett's cloud-muddled scum
why take a photo? – it's horizontal everything, grey grit and glum
boundless flatness, no margins to licence light for sky or shore
just a single buck in the wetland waging a breath-taking cold war.
Binoculars numb as ice, we tramp home, exonerated and wet
our brands well water-logged: Peregrine, Plover, Shelduck. Avocet.

**Worldwide Worship**

You never knew devotion could be quite so diverting
MILFs, Mature, Spanking and Squirting
yet all the disciples are strangely alluring
agog at the man-god's golden-calf offering
they offer steadfast, selfless, veneration
articulate lip-service and adulation
though you have to ask a little bit
*What the fuck do they get out of it?*

contort, so every angle of devotion
can be a close-up focus on holy communion
HD stubble and BBC implanting
purple-gashed breasts and paperclip piercing
they pray upside-down, standing, kneeling or sitting
holy waters spurt out like dribbling cake icing
though you have to ask a little bit
*What the fuck do they get out of it?*

the order of worship is always identical
the poses regulated, all ecstasies theatrical
no coffees, pee-breaks or anything obstetrical
just Stocking, Small Tit, Aunty and Anal
surely nothing in the world of human liturgy
has quite so many crazy cult categories
though you have to ask a little bit
*What the fuck do they get out of it?*

it's rite on trend for every hair to be shorn
to show-off your hymns/hers as patio, not lawn
whether British, Brazilian, Lithuanian or Leprechaun
we must revere the pink tunnel, adore the pink prawn
and the rule of ritual that trumps all the rest
is to come sacramentally over Tupperware breasts
though you have to ask a little bit
*What the fuck do they get out of it?*

for every X-crotch star, every A-list penetrant
are worshipped worldwide by a billion celebrants

solo pilgrims sacrificing blood, flesh and bone
an international throng praying in bedrooms alone
this new congregation has one universal aim
to inventively martyr themselves again and again
though you have to ask a little bit
*What the fuck?*

## Scrot at the back

Rescued from some corrugated iron gulag
your face deadpan, poultry eye blank
a Misérable awaiting the next attack
left for dead by a roadside carjack
let's see how it goes, my rag & bone girl
this is a bitch-eat-bitch henpeck world
I can't protect you from the coop flak
but I'll give you a name, 'Scrot at the back'.

I'm looking for the faintest whisper of soul
but you're under North Korean cage control
eyes so watchful, you've never had pride
only a concretized countryside
feathers plucked off your neck and arse
you're a bald-bum cluck, threadbare sparse
elbows an oven-ready chicken-wing snack
but I'll give you a name, 'Scrot at the back'.

Can't recognise strawberries, crusts of bread
nothing registers but the crap you were fed
chicken chicken, you cower from commotion
terror is your only surviving emotion
it's lynch law here, my featherless Scrot
I should wring your neck before you rot
but I'll feed you a special mouth-watering snack
You're the only hen named. Scrot at the back.

## This is the useless

This is the useless useless thing about everything
the pointless point of nothing daily nothing
the time of day the day of time drearily drearing
the hour then the hour then the hour of breathing
the rolling from bed washing tea-ing coffee-ing
the getting up from TV full of nothing nothing
the empty whiplash of everything blaring blaring
the going to bed without undressing washing caring
the same old things in the world happening happening
the empty television talkers moaning moaning
the poodle politicians saying nothing nothing
the weather sweating damp clouds bleating cursing
the minutes threatening stroke cancer death dying
the effort of thinking the effort of not crying
the dead parents disappearing writhing writhing
the useless purpose of living and dying.

## Bunker (this is knowledge you can never know)

We drop down lanes, hedges, black mulch
dead-end dirt, gullies, battlefields' necrose
skid tyres in shit, grip grit, follow our gypsy nose
till we find the gate, welded tight, industrial high
a big man scowls, belches, elbows us inside

choppers meticulously set on the moss tarmac
men locked around a rusted hull
cursed cars, cache of campervans, a cadaver skull
sodden sofas guard armoured iron doors
bombproof concrete from the second world war

with a nod, half smirk/thumb jerk, we're inside
the bunker – dark, warm, fat slap shoulder
peering through steam, tequila, odour
beer, beards, back-patch leather jackets
bass beating bravado from our breadbaskets

the chosen few - muscle, guts, cigarette tar
cocaine, spliffs, disembowelled guitar
bomb for bomb bombarding the soul
heavy metal torn from an alien arsehole
the gift of gang. Brotherhood. No control.

No wine-bar whingeing into microphones
or Grayson grovelling Wendy House woes
no dribble-piss poems or I'm-a-prick prose.
No, this is knowledge you can never know
this is knowledge you can never know.

## He

Someone

tailors his ties, valets his yacht
chauffeurs his cars, purloins his pot
reserves his restaurants, taxis his jets
smooths his sheets, cheques his assets
kits out his kitchens, Botoxes his skin
massages his back, shaves his chin
manicures his mail, warms his featherbed
sorts out his socials, sweet-talks his head
bids for his art, decorates his house
steams his shirts, shoots his grouse
harvests his grapes, chefs his food
diagnoses his disposition, medicates his mood
weeds his lawns, rakes his gravel drive
MRIs him annually to keep him alive.

He

does nothing himself, never lifts a hand
he is a self-made modern selfie man.

## Auntie and Drills

*I've looked at drills from both sides now*
*From up and down and still somehow*
*It's drill's illusions I recall*
*I really don't know drills at all.*

This is the way of drills
Auntie don't dirty her hands with skills
no De Wault dramas, Hitachi or Ryobi
soft focus Makita, Bosch, Milwaukee
she claims any colour drill is willin
but as you and I know
not all drills are good at drillin

She puts it out that all drills are capable
but some don't drill brick, it's inescapable
plastic gears made in the Far East or China
pretty handgrips for the interior designer
she claims every chuck and Harry is willin
but as you and I know
they ain't man enuf for drillin

What does Auntie know of torque control
she's happier with opining and vox pop polls
illusional drills, mock motors posing
as Japanese/German SDS engineering
she claims every bit is willin
but as you and I know
not all bits cut it at drillin

Every blinkin brand gotta get a mention
all plugged in for viewers' attention
none of these motors will be enduring
any rubbish drill gets her DIY umpiring
she claims anything cordless is willin
but as you and I know
it's not Auntie that does the drillin

no, Auntie could never make a canoe

she don't even know which way to turn a screw
has to get a man to undo the chuck
order the maid to Dyson-up the muck
eats her scones, displays her virtues
thinks the drillin is done in high-heel shoes.

## Hoarders

Welcome to Buckingham's bargain-basement, have a delve
we've stacks of shiny salvers on our silver-service shelves
piles of posh pots dipso-diplomats donated to one's self
juggernaut jewels, bent ivory, wide-eyed animal pelts
God knows what's at the back of these cavernous caves
a heap of forgotten stuff that's no longer the rage.

Welcome to Windsor's whisky-wrecked wings
this is where we keep a shit-load of shiny things
gallows gold, crapulent crowns, a room of ruby rings
a cellar of dodgy booze Johnny Foreigner brings
Château Lafite, Dom Pérignon, fancy flasks of gin
a pile of prezzies we need to sort through and sling.

Welcome to Sandringham's cigar-smoked cellars
here our paintings lie deep in sedimentary layers
Leonardos, Picassos, Stubbs, unwanted Vermeers
it's become a humongous pileup over the years
a crush of canvas crusted in crap and spiders' nests
we should take it to the dump with all the rest.

Welcome to the Kensington kleptomaniac keep
here we store a shitload of books we never read
can't flog em, can't give em away, dross we don't need
candelabras, intaglios, Fabergé eggs you can't even eat
mounds of muck that's built up and will never rot
a ton of stuff we don't even know we've got.

Welcome to the Balmoral Bacchanalian ballroom
there's so much paraphernalia strewn here in the gloom
I've never been down those crypts but I'm assured
it's where the best gear, the good shit, is sorted and stored
it's lain there for centuries, worm-eaten and ignored
old Brueghel's, Monet's, rusted maces and swords.

Welcome to Holyrood's halberdier warehousing
here there's a shedload of furs that need delousing
old Canova's, Sèvres, chipped Chelsea and things

you should see all the clobber crammed into the wings
junk we ought to take to the boot sale to tout
fill the Roller with jumble, have a good clear-out.

Hoarders? Well, come to our cosy private quarters
a modest room where we hide from reporters
here we eruct, watch The Crown, make cheese on toast
heat Heinz beans and spaghetti, eat our Sunday roast.
No, we're not hoarders, magpies or squirrels in our dreys
it's not one's fault there's just too much stuff nowadays.

## A Poet Fits a Toilet

It's all about words, innit, easy as shit
stick me dick in the dictionary, dipshit
then a quick wank of words, submit bullshit
become a prize-winning poet, a Bloodaxe hit
then you're the Oxford Prostate Professor of Lit

meanwhile I've got to fit this lady's unit
naturally, the cold feed pipe don't fit
gotta bend 15-mil copper, solder it
chop out the wall, fill and tile a bit
everything's a misfit, a bloomin retrofit

there's no overflow, needa cistern identikit
and the stench pipe is a right old tar pit
plastic to cast-iron, it's gonna crack and split
those tiles she bought won't never fit
I'm knackered, look at me sweaty armpit

mind you, she herself, she ain't half fit
proffering profiteroles in her posh outfit
she's got a smashing pair of double-knits
I'd love to share her banana split
fire us both into turbocharged orbit

(yeah...but she'd probably do a Bobbitt
a gill-slit moonlit, chick-flit skit)
can't see nothing in this damn cockpit
electric's dead, bathroom's unlit
plaster's coming off, I could throw a fit

toilet weighs a ton, I should just quit
elbows in water, kneeling on grit
Brit? Work permit? Lickety split
busting me balls peddling plumber's wit
but she thinks I'm Brexit, this job is the pits

my hands are buggered, stuck in this slit
I need some O'Keeffe's to protect me mitts

and where the fuck is my drill bit?
all this for writing no editor will git
a magazine wankerous and counterfeit

bunged-up rectums pretending to be 'it'
hiding behind opaque feely-feely shit
those writers are fake, you have to admit
they're poncy plumber cowboy misfits
their words are b-anal, truth-scratching nits

I'm gonna have to take another hit
while I'm down here, squashing me man-tits
spin the lady of the house some new bullshit
what the hell do I do now, the toilet's in bits
had a skinful last night, bloody daft twit

there's one political truth and this is it:
When you need a shit, you need a shit.

## Spider Women

This is the time of the year when
under evening's vapour and purple air
days discard the sun, grass fails, underfed, shrubs are starkers.
Here, in the stalks and branches, the ladies hang out

floating sticky lines upon breezes, they parachute the wind
unearthing hidden traumas, psychological tripwires
lassoing strands across sham canyons
weaving femme-fatale webs.

Disremembering, they rent revenge, will-o'-the-wisp night stalkers
solidarity gives them licence to store their mother's cobwebs
spit silk, engender death
maim, bite, decapitate.

Ninjutsu, they weave a million lines
daring men to trespass for sex
they pounce, tie them down, finger their faces with ghost-webs
stamp them with domestic violence.

Risk going behind the shed to split logs, sweat, your femur swearing
to fuel their living room fire
and they will catch your face, tease your masculine gaucherie
wrap your body in torpor

craving you to be cruel, to inseminate their groups.
They drop men's drunken sorrows and tired bodies
from their webs, female feeding female
with torn legs and gossamer threads

asking:
How do I feel?
How do I feel?
How do I feel?

## Cover-up

They have scraped the skin off the earth
slumbering seeds, weeds, dandelion turf
all flora and fauna, the whole tree of life
leatherjacket, worm, millipede, woodlice
a merciless mechanical mass extinction
a permanent maintenance-free solution

to compact, cover-up with hard-core
scalpings pounded into the outdoor floor
all is horizontal, perpendicular, a despot designer
a cement showroom for the garden hardliner
slabs stolen from a Yorkshire quarry at dawn
a factory-farmed neon checkerboard lawn.

She has scraped the soul off her face
freckles, pimples, pores, all will be replaced
the topsoil of the skin, all must be peeled
any wrinkle, pucker, blemish – filled, concealed
a chemical methodical mass extinction
a never-lasting high-maintenance solution.

## Joy

No seagull jumbo jets
these are the stunt planes
micro-lights, scimitar-winged
fly-by-wire fighter pilots
chiselling the grass

forcing up the joy stick
careering without care
they hurtle, roller coast
g-force, swerve beyond swerve
daredevil darts

pitching fast bouncers at the grass
they shear sheer air
daggers drawn at dawn
big-mouthing antennae, abdomen et al
fine-tuned hell raisers.

If at any stage in life you find yourself
warm-wined, balconied on dry French oak
dropping pistachio shells on rough-cut floorboards
will there always be the swallows pillaging
zipping the skin of the swimming pool

threading eyes with joy
through the eye of the needle
into stone-cracked spider barns
their youths, cocky, yellow-mouthed
cemented in their pouches

screaming:
Let me fly, let me fly, let me fly.

## Poem for a Lady

Lady Benz
there's something in your voluminous white flanks
your cavernous capacity, bonnet to Bundesbank
your three-point show-off star emblem
that signals breakdowns ain't your problem
superiority, infotainment, innovation
I'm all up for your German domination.

Lady Benz
your pleasing perfume, turning on your ignition
I'm glue-sniffing your tyres, 9G-TRONIC transmission
electric is pathetic, but with your Euro 6 engine
(and catalytic green emission reduction)
I'd cream every Vauxhall, Renault and Volkswagen
from the muddy Severn to the Welsh Wye dragon.

Lady Benz
one day I'll get off this maniacal M4
stop delivering to cunts on front doors
I'll throw in a mattress, stick a carpet on the floor
and crash out of this lug-logistics World-War
I'll go camper-vanning, the whole of the island
England and Wales, but not eff'ing Scotland.

Lady Benz
I'm breaking your rear springs loading your back
drinking Earl Grey tea with treacle flapjack
I'm packing treasures - Shakespeare, Brompton
Daiwa, Shimano, Penn, Hardy and Moulton.
So sod poets and bullshitters and Harold Pinter
all I want for Christmas is an artic white Sprinter.

Printed in Great Britain
by Amazon

17284917R00098